Praise for *Found*

"Curtis Martin and Edward Sri have provided us a high quality and readily accessible resource for cultivating disciples among the people of the Church and our wider communities. We need to find new ways of bringing the Gospel to the contemporary world and new ways to proclaim the truth of God's love for each one of us. We need to help men and women to be ministers of welcome, encouragement, and reconciliation. Conversion of heart often follows from watching others practice their faith and then embracing a way of life they see as possible. May this book help you to hear your call, to come to a greater knowledge of the love Jesus has for you and to go forth in sharing that grace and blessing with others."

— Seán Cardinal O'Malley, O.F.M. Cap., *Archbishop of Boston*

"For over twenty years, the evangelizing work of FOCUS has inspired the Church. At its heart is a serious commitment to formation, and with this timely book Curtis Martin and Edward Sri, two passionate evangelizers, bring the proven formation tools of FOCUS to a wider audience. May those equipped for mission through these pages help win, build, and send a new generation of disciples for the Lord."

— Most Rev. John O. Barres, S.T.D., J.C.L., D.D., *Bishop of Rockville Centre*

"*Foundations for Discipleship* offers a practical guide to participating in the master work of evangelization given to us by Pope St. Paul VI in *Evangelii Nuntiandi*. Curtis Martin and Edward Sri invite everyone to encounter Christ, deepen the experience of him and then witness to him in the activities of daily life. The kerygma and its proclamation come alive in the pages of this book, which I recommend to all who are eager to mature in their faith and share it with others."

— Most Rev. Timothy P. Broglio, *Archbishop for the Military Services, USA*

"Each time I encounter a FOCUS missionary or attend one of their events, I come away encouraged about the future of our Church. Their work at universities across the country is a fruitful response to our Lord's call to 'go and make disciples.' For this reason, I am most grateful for their new book, which will be an indispensable resource for any layperson passionate about evangelization."

— Most Rev. William E. Lori, *Archbishop of Baltimore*

"*Foundations for Discipleship* powerfully articulates the successful ministry model of evangelization used by Jesus and applies it to our modern age. Each chapter succinctly captures the beauty and the attractiveness of the Gospel message in a way that can help missionary disciples more effectively invest and multiply the gift of faith. Every disciple of Jesus can benefit from reading, studying and sharing this text."

— Most Rev. Daniel H. Mueggenborg, *Auxiliary Bishop of Seattle*

"As a new apostolic age breaks upon us, few movements of the Holy Spirit have done as much to build a genuine culture of missionary discipleship in the Church as FOCUS. This book, solid and practical, spells out beautifully the transformative vision which has already brought forth such impressive witness and genuine holiness in so many lives. Reading these pages, I know it for sure: there's much more to come!"

— Monsignor James P. Shea, *President, the University of Mary*

"FOCUS has long been a leader in training people in the art of discipleship. Until now, a detailed and written account of their model of how to be a disciple of Jesus and how to walk with others in discipleship has not been widely available to the general public. These discipleship articles are groundbreaking in their ability to communicate the simple yet profound art of discipleship."

— Fr. Mike Schmitz, *Director of Youth and Young Adult Ministry, Diocese of Duluth, and Chaplain, University of Minnesota-Duluth Newman Center*

"The ideas of discipleship and evangelization are not second-nature to the people in the parish, even the ones who are most committed. I'm so thankful that there is finally a very practical resource like this to lead parishioners to a deeper encounter with Jesus Christ and train them in the basic skills of evangelization. Through these easy-to-use articles, parishioners are not only growing personally in prayer and holiness — they are training others to accompany, evangelize, and live as missionary disciples themselves."

— Fr. John Jirak, *Pastor and Vicar for Evangelization,*
Discipleship, and Stewardship, Diocese of Wichita

"Spiritual poverty runs rampant in many of our communities; and while our catechetical content is improving, many Catholics are still missing that strong sense of discipleship with the living, risen Lord Jesus. *Foundations for Discipleship* is a treasure trove of time-tested ways to approach the essential ministries of evangelization and discipleship. By God's grace and mercy, this resource will lead many people of faith to a deeper connection with Christ — living out that discipleship in full communion with his body, the Church."

— Ken Ogorek, *Director of Catechesis, Archdiocese of Indianapolis*

"Rooted in the Gospel and the Church's wisdom, FOCUS shares its effective yet practical approach to evangelization. Our parishes, schools, and communities will benefit from this proven method that is "modeled by the Master" and adapted for today's disciples. *Foundations for Discipleship* is a welcome addition to the toolbox of anyone serious about living his or her baptismal call to the fullest."

— Edward P. Herrera, *Director,*
Office of Marriage and Family Life, Archdiocese of Baltimore

"Few things in life are more important than working shoulder to shoulder with other disciples who are striving to follow Jesus and tell others about him. *Foundations for Discipleship* is a fantastic resource to help you live out this way of life. Start reading it today; better yet, grab some people you know and dive in together."

— Kevin Cotter, *Executive Director, Amazing Parish*

"Foundations of Discipleship is transforming our parish culture into a culture of mission. These training resources have helped so many of our parishioners, staff, and clergy live as true missionary disciples in their daily lives. People are more confident and equipped to share the Faith and are bringing their evangelistic passion into all areas of parish life — over coffee, in their families, in conversations with parents after school, in various ministries and small groups. And most of all, these ordinary lay leaders aren't just evangelizers. They are training others to go out and share the Gospel themselves."

— Fr. Matt Foley, *Pastor, Archdiocese of Chicago*

"Foundations for Discipleship has definitely helped me to grow as a priest and pastor of souls. This intentional approach to making missionary disciples grounds me in the Gospel mandate of Christ; and even in the midst of administrative cares and other temporal concerns of parish life, it helps me to always be mindful of what all of this is about: the salvation of souls for the glorious majesty of God."

— Fr. Jeffrey Lewis, *Pastor, Diocese of Spokane*

"Oftentimes I encounter faithful Catholics and parish staff members who want to equip people to be missionary disciples, but they simply don't know how. *Foundations for Discipleship* is the perfect playbook to use stories and short articles to lead people into a deeper relationship with Christ and to equip them to be disciple-makers. We remember stories. We learn from stories. Even Jesus taught through stories. Since reading this book, I have used several of these articles in my own ministry to guide people deeper in their walk with Jesus."

— Andrea Patch, *Managing Director of Evangelization and Catechesis, Archdiocese of Cincinnati*

"As a layperson working for the Church, I always look for good and faithful resources to inspire and motivate me to form missionary disciples. *Foundations for Discipleship* provides any faithful Catholic with the tools they need to guide others through the process of Win, Build, and Send. I highly recommend this book to anyone striving to live mission in their everyday lives."

— Lauren Garcia, *Communications and Outreach Specialist, Nebraska Catholic Conference*

NIHIL OBSTAT: Tomas Fuerte, S.T.L.
                 Censor Librorum

IMPRIMATUR: +Most Reverend Samuel J. Aquila, S.T.L.
                 Archbishop of Denver
                 Denver, Colorado, USA
                 November 24, 2020

EDITORS: Curtis Martin and Edward Sri

ASSOCIATE EDITORS: Stephanie Parks and Travis Todd

CONTRIBUTORS: Curtis Martin, Edward Sri, Travis Todd, Stephanie Parks, Kevin Cotter, and John Bishop

ADVISORS: John Zimmer, Dan Krebsbach, Marcus Schoch, Hilary Draftz, Dominic Paolucci, Daniel Paris, Shannon Zurcher, Carrie Wagner, Erin Scanlan, Brian McAdam, Jessica Navin, Sarah Akers, Levi Rash, Tony Menke, Vince Sartori, James Dunnigan, Mark Joseph, Brock Martin, Jane Voelker, JohnMarc Skoch, Brendon Pond, Joseph Gruenwald, and Tyler Degen

ACKNOWLEDGEMENTS:

Thank you to the 100+ FOCUS missionaries who gave extensive feedback on these articles.

Special thanks to The Little J Marketing Co. for their work on the interior layout design; Christina Eberle for her copyediting work throughout this project; and Amy Frazier for her work on the interior graphic design.

Thank you to our catechetical and theological advisors: Doug Bushman, Ben Akers, and Lucas Pollice.

FOUNDATIONS FOR DISCIPLESHIP

Curtis Martin & Edward Sri

EDITORS

TABLE OF CONTENTS

i   **Preface:** *The Church's Vision for Evangelization and Discipleship*

FOUNDATIONS FOR DISCIPLESHIP

02   **Leader's Introduction:** *Transformative Discipleship*

WIN

14   **WIN: FOR THE LEADER**

17   **ENCOUNTER**
18   1.0 | Something More
30   1.1 | God's Fatherly Love

39   **THE GOSPEL**
40   2.0 | The Gospel

BUILD

54   **BUILD: FOR THE LEADER**

57   **ACTS 2:42**
58   3.0 | "In the Dust of the Rabbi": Living as a Disciple of Jesus
68   3.1 | Prayer: Spiritual Breathing
78   3.2 | Fellowship: Virtuous Friendships
88   3.3 | Sacraments: The Eucharist
96   3.4 | Sacraments: The Healing Power of Confession
106   3.5 | The Apostles' Teaching: The Battle for Your Mind

115 THE HIGH CALL TO MISSION

116 4.0 | Moral Authority and "The Big 3"

132 4.1 | Faithfulness to Christ and His Church

140 4.2 | The High Call to Mission

SEND

152 **SEND: FOR THE LEADER**

155 **MISSION FORMATION**

156 5.0 | A Vision for Missionary Discipleship: Win-Build-Send

172 5.1 | Incarnational Evangelization: The Art of Accompaniment

182 5.2 | The Power of Your Testimony

190 5.3 | Leading a Transformative Bible Study

202 5.4 | Sharing the Gospel: A Call to Conversion

212 5.5 | Walking With Others in Discipleship

223 **PERSONAL FORMATION**

224 6.0 | Pursuing Christlike Character

234 6.1 | Deeper Prayer: Persevering in Love

244 6.2 | Works of Mercy

252 6.3 | Intercessory Prayer

260 6.4 | "Take Up Your Cross and Follow Me": Embracing the Cross in Mission

PREFACE

The Church's Vision for Evangelization and Discipleship

The Catholic Church emphasizes the call to evangelization, discipleship, and missionary discipleship. But what does it all mean? And what does it look like in real life — in one's parish, diocese, family, or personal apostolate?

While there's a lot of talk about these themes, it's crucial that they be grounded in the Catholic Church's magisterial teachings on evangelization. From Vatican II to Pope Francis, the Church identifies key moments in the journey of Christian discipleship: from initially encountering Christ and surrendering one's life to him, to deepening one's adherence to Christ and his Church, to being sent on mission in evangelizing others. One easy way to see these three key moments in the journey of discipleship is through Pope St. Paul VI's apostolic exhortation *Evangelization in the Modern World*[1] (*Evangelii Nuntiandi*, 1975) and the recent *Directory for Catechesis* from the Pontifical Council of the New Evangelization[2] (2020).

First, according to these and other magisterial teachings, there are two essential ways we are to evangelize: through our living *witness* and through *explicit proclamation* of the Gospel (EN 21–22; *Directory* 31, 33, 37).

Second, when someone has welcomed the Gospel into their lives, we want to help their initial faith take deeper root by cultivating the basics of Christian living, an "apprenticeship in the Christian life" that fosters an ever-deeper adherence to Christ (*Directory* 34, cf. *Directory* 31, EN 23).

Third, as disciples of Jesus grow in the Faith, we also want to invite and train them to live their mission to evangelize others, for every true disciple of Jesus is also a missionary disciple (EN 24; *Directory*, 31, 40).

There are many ways one can describe these three key stages of accompanying souls on the journey of Christian discipleship. In FOCUS we have found it helpful to refer to them simply as "Win-Build-Send": we endeavor to "win" people to Christ and the Church by sharing the Gospel with our witness and our words. We help "build" them up in living the Faith through prayer, fellowship, the sacraments, and the teachings of the Church (Acts 2:42). And we train them to be "sent" on mission to evangelize others.

While the articles contained in this book may at times use certain expressions particular to FOCUS, the central ideas and approaches themselves are not the creative exercise of any one individual or organization. They are rooted in the Catholic tradition and magisterial teaching on evangelization, catechesis, and pastoral ministry from Vatican II, Pope St. Paul VI, Pope St. John Paul II, Pope Benedict XVI, and Pope Francis. They point to the way of life for *all* Catholics — clergy, religious, pastoral leaders, teachers, catechists, parents, and ordinary lay people — since all the baptized are called to live as true missionary disciples. As the *Directory of Catechesis* explains, "Every one of the baptized, in so far as he is a 'missionary disciple,' is an active participant in this ecclesial mission" (40).

Here is a brief overview of the Discipleship Articles in this book and how they relate to the Church's vision for evangelization and discipleship.

WIN

WITNESS (THE FOUNDATION)

"Above all the Gospel must be proclaimed by witness." (*EN 21*)

More important than any faith formation program, resource, or study is the living witness of the individuals using those tools. The same is true with the Discipleship Articles contained in this book. These are tools that can assist you in your work of evangelization and discipleship, but they can't replace you. You are the primary instrument God wants to use in the process of evangelization, which is why you must be living the truths in these resources before teaching them. If we endeavor to serve as missionary disciples, we must be disciples first.

Paul VI reminds us that the first step in evangelization is our living witness, the "silent proclamation" of the Gospel (EN 21). Our lived example in the Faith inspires others to want what we have: "Through the wordless witness these Christians stir up irresistible questions in the hearts of those who see how they live: Why are they like this? Why do they live in this way? What or who is it that inspires them? Why are they in our midst?" (EN 21).

This is why Pope Francis challenges all of us to renew our own personal encounter with Christ, for all that we do on mission flows from that encounter.[3] The more we ourselves are living deeply from that encounter and the foundational habits of the earliest disciples — prayer, fellowship, sacraments, and forming our minds with the teachings of Christ (cf. Acts 2:42) — the more the Holy Spirit can work through us so that every person we meet encounters not just us, but Jesus radiating through us.

EXPLICIT PROCLAMATION (ARTICLES 1.0 – 2.0)

"There is no true evangelization if the name, the teaching, the life, the promises, the kingdom and the mystery of Jesus of Nazareth, the Son of God, are not proclaimed." (EN 22)

As foundational as our living witness may be, witness alone is not enough. It "always remains insufficient," Paul VI explains. "Even the finest witness will prove ineffective in the long run if it is not explained, justified … and made explicit by a clear and unequivocal proclamation of the Lord Jesus" (EN 22). Proclaiming the Gospel with our words is essential in the work of evangelization.

To help you prepare someone to receive this proclamation of the Gospel and to till the soil of their hearts, the first articles in this book (Articles 1.0 – 1.1) focus on the love of Jesus and mercy of God the Father. These basic articles are options that can help you have initial conversations about the Faith with those who have not yet been evangelized. This will help prepare someone to receive the explicit proclamation of the Gospel.

Many Christians, however, are unsure about how to make this explicit proclamation. They may never have heard the Gospel message presented in a clear and personal way that inspired them to surrender their lives to Christ. They may have never heard the key points of the Gospel message — what the Church calls the "kerygma" — spelled out for them and presented in an authentically Catholic way (see *Directory* 57 – 60). Others might be uncertain how to share the Gospel message naturally with someone. What do I say? How do I say it? What are the main points? How do I do this and not sound awkward or pushy?

This is why we've included an article entitled "The Gospel." This resource makes it easy for you to have an ordinary conversation with someone about the one thing that matters most in life: Jesus Christ and his loving work of salvation for us. It also helps you invite someone to make Jesus and the Catholic Faith the center of their life. This article is just one approach to proclaiming the Gospel message — there are, of course, other authentically Catholic approaches one might take — but it's one we've found helpful to ensure the kerygma is proclaimed in an effective way.

This is an important part of the process of conversion. According to Catholic magisterial teaching on evangelization and catechesis, this is the goal of evangelization: to inspire someone to "say 'yes' to Jesus,"[4] to be "fervent in their faith and in Christian living"[5] and to take on a "profound Christian outlook" on life.[6] Sometimes, however, faith formation programs, Bible studies, retreats, and conferences skip this important step and assume people have already been evangelized, which is not something we can do today.[7]

One other point worth noting: All other articles continue to call people to a deeper conversion, inviting them into an ever-deeper encounter with this foundational Gospel message. While this initial sharing of the Gospel is often called "Primary Proclamation," it is not called "primary" merely because it is first in the order of other topics that need to be proclaimed. It's called primary because, as Pope Francis explains, it is first in importance and is foundational for every other aspect of faith formation.[8] Whether we're teaching on prayer, the Bible, virtue, the Eucharist, or Catholic social teaching, we must always bring the catechetical point back to the message of God's amazing love for us. The message that God has a plan for our lives — that even though we turned away from him in sin, he still mercifully sought us out, sent his Son who lovingly gave up his life for our sins and then rose again and sent his Spirit to us through his Church so that we can be reunited with him — is a story that needs to be told over and over again. That story never grows old. Everything we believe and do as Catholics is bound up with that story. A Christian who has become bored with that story has probably lost his first love (cf. Rv 2:4).

BUILD

PROGRAM OF LIFE (ARTICLES 3.0 – 3.5)

"[P]roclamation only reaches full development when it is listened to, accepted and assimilated, and when it arouses a genuine adherence in the one who has thus received it. Adherence to the truths which the Lord in his mercy has revealed; still more, an adherence to a program of life — a life henceforth transformed." (EN 23)

Saying "yes" to Jesus and the Gospel is a turning point in one's life, but it is just the beginning of the life of a disciple. That initial "yes" needs to take root in one's soul and to shape the person's entire life. St. Paul VI emphasizes the word "adherence" here. The disciple must *adhere* to Jesus Christ, to the truth Christ revealed, to the Church, to the sacraments. It's like the disciple enters a "new world" and adheres to a whole "new manner of being, of living and of living in community" (EN 23).

This process of discipleship and transformation does not happen automatically. It needs to be learned. That's why the next several Discipleship Articles focus on what it means to be a disciple of Jesus and the four key practices of a disciple as found in the early Church, namely prayer, fellowship, the sacraments, and the teachings of the apostles (Acts 2:42) (Articles 3.0 – 3.5). These are the key habits to which the earliest disciples devoted themselves and are the best guide for helping shape the rhythm of one's life with Christ.

THE HIGH CALL: INVITATION TO A NEW APOSTOLATE (ARTICLES 4.0 – 4.2)

"[T]he presentation of the Gospel message is not an optional contribution for the Church. It is the duty incumbent on her by the command of the Lord Jesus, so that people can believe and be saved ... It is a question of people's salvation ... It merits having the apostle consecrate to it all his time and all his energies, and to sacrifice for it, if necessary, his own life." (EN 5)

Evangelization is not an extra, optional task for the Christian disciple. It's a way of life that flows from our identity in Christ. Anyone who has truly encountered Christ, who has experienced his love, his mercy, and his saving power, cannot help but want to share Christ with others: "[I]t is unthinkable that someone should accept the Word and give himself to the kingdom without becoming a person who bears witness to it and proclaims it in his turn" (EN 24). Indeed, the person who is truly evangelized "goes on to evangelize others" (EN 24). Similarly, Pope Francis says that a true disciple is always a missionary disciple, participating in the Church's mission to share Christ with others.[9]

There are diverse ways to call people to live missionary discipleship in the Church. One approach we've found helpful is to give an explicit invitation to live out their duty as baptized Catholics to evangelize. Oftentimes, when people are not given a vision for what evangelization and missionary discipleship can look like and a specific invitation to lead others, sharing the Faith is not a priority and the urgency of the Gospel does not sink in as deeply. Unless the call to evangelize is made clear, Christians are not likely to say with St. Paul, "Woe to me if I do not preach the Gospel" (1 Cor 9:16). But with the right vision, a specific invitation and some basic practical training, Christian disciples are more likely to give their lives generously to the work of evangelization and help lead more souls to Christ's kingdom.

The next set of Discipleship Articles in this book is centered around that invitation — what we describe as the High Call to Mission. It is the High Call not only to love Christ, but also to love his mission and to endeavor to satiate his thirst for souls. It is the High Call to use one's life not for one's own purposes but for God's in service of his kingdom.

How does one share the vision of evangelization in an inspiring way? That's what the "High Call" article will help you do (Article 4.2). The related articles preceding the High Call to Mission, entitled "Moral Authority and the 'Big 3'" and "Faithfulness to Christ and His Church," are essential for any Christian disciple but especially important so as to represent Christ and his Church faithfully in the work of evangelization (Articles 4.0 – 4.2).

SEND

THE MISSION: TRAINING FOR A NEW APOSTOLATE (ARTICLES 5.0 – 6.4)

"A serious preparation is needed for all workers of evangelization." (EN 73)

The work of evangelization and forming missionary disciples comes with a tremendous responsibility. We are not merely running programs; we are helping to care for souls — and not just the souls of the people we directly serve, but also the souls they may touch through their own evangelization efforts. That's why we want to prepare missionary disciples carefully to be effective in accompanying others and leading the people *they* serve to take the next steps of faith in their walk with the Lord.

The "Send" Discipleship Articles focus on some key elements of that training, including how to give a testimony (see EN 41); how to share the Gospel (see EN

42); the importance of small faith communities and how to lead a small group (EN 58); the primacy of "person-to-person" ministry based on authentic friendship, giving "not only the Gospel but our very selves" (1 Thes 2:8; EN 46, 79); how all mission flows from the interior life and the Holy Spirit as "the principal agent of evangelization" (EN 75); and how to use resources that give a basic formation aimed at forming Christian patterns of living (EN 44). Other articles touch on continual personal formation that strengthens our witness, including topics such as pursuing virtue, the works of mercy, going deeper in prayer, interceding for the souls we serve, and conforming our lives to the cross (Articles 6.0 – 6.4). This is not an exhaustive list of training topics, but it does include some key elements for forming missionary disciples.

Most of all, the articles in this section cast vision for forming missionary disciples — how to lead people to an *encounter* with Christ, how to *accompany* them as they deepen their union with Christ in their daily lives, and how to prepare others to become *Spirit-filled evangelizers* themselves.[10] St. Paul VI explains how Jesus chose disciples, trained them and then sent them (EN 66). We imitate Jesus as we endeavor to "win" people to Christ and the Church; we help "build" them up in living the Faith through prayer, fellowship, the sacraments, and the teachings of the Church; and then we train them to be "sent" on mission to evangelize others.

Notes

[1] Paul VI, *Evangelii Nuntiandi*, Vatican.va.

[2] Pontifical Council for the Promotion of the New Evangelization. *Directory for Catechesis* (USCCB: Washington, 2020).

[3] Francis, *Evangelii Gaudium*, accessed November 3, 2020, Vatican.va, 3

[4] John Paul II, *Catechesi Tradendae,* accessed November 4, 2020, Vatican.va, 20.

[5] John Paul II, *Redemptoris Missio,* accessed November 2, 2020, Vatican.va, 33.

[6] Congregation for the Clergy, *General Directory for Catechesis,* accessed November 4, 2020, Vatican.va, 58.

[7] John Paul II, *Catechesi Tradendae,* accessed November 4, 2020, Vatican.va, 19.

[8] Francis, *Evangelii Gaudium*, accessed November 6, 2020, Vatican.va, 164.

[9] Ibid., 120.

[10] Ibid., 259.

Notes

FOUNDATIONS FOR DISCIPLESHIP

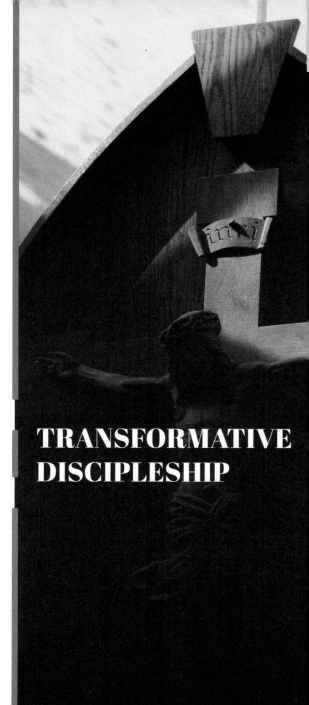

LEADER'S INTRODUCTION

TRANSFORMATIVE DISCIPLESHIP

I n In the early 1940s, the Nazis dominated many countries in central Europe. And they were not neutral toward religion.

They sought to destroy the Catholic Church, sending thousands of priests and religious to concentration camps, silencing any opposition from religious leaders, prohibiting most public expressions of faith, and outlawing education in the Christian life. The goal was to prevent the Faith from being passed on to the younger generation and to indoctrinate young people in the Nazi ideology at school, in the media, and in government-sponsored activities.

In this time of crisis, some laypeople heroically stepped up to lead underground groups and pass on the Faith to the youth. One man named Jan Tyranowski led one of the most successful of these clandestine ministries with college-aged men, calling them Living Rosary groups.

Jan was a tailor in Nazi-ruled Poland. He was not a priest and had no formal training in theology. But at the risk of his own life, he opened his apartment to several young men to instruct them in the spiritual life and train them to form Living Rosary groups of their own with their peers. He was intentional in his ministry, reinforcing the basics of the Faith and helping the men take the next steps in their relationship with Christ. He taught them how to root out sin, go deeper in prayer and discern God's will. He opened up for them the beauty of the Rosary and the wisdom of the saints. He also trained them for mission, sending them to reach their peers with the Gospel.

The world may have never known Pope John Paul II if it wasn't for the discipleship of Jan Tyranowski.

His underground ministry had such a profound effect that ten of the men involved went on to become priests. One of those priests was someone named Karol Wojtyła, the man who eventually became Pope St. John Paul II — the pope who had such a tremendous influence on the Church and the world.

That's the impact one ordinary Christian can have when they pour their life into accompanying others in Christian discipleship and mission. Venerable Jan Tyranowski may be one of the most influential people of the 20th century. It's not because he rose to wealth, fame, or power. It's not for any great accomplishment that will ever be featured on CNN or secure a Nobel Prize. Rather, Jan simply invested himself personally in a few good men, leading them to encounter Christ at a deeper level and training them to go out and do the same for others. And those men went on to do great things, playing a crucial role in helping to preserve Catholic culture in Poland in a time of crisis. The world may have never known Pope St. John Paul II if it wasn't for the missionary discipleship of Jan Tyranowski.

―――――――――――――――――――― **DISCUSS** ――――――――――――――――

What inspires you about the example of Venerable Jan Tyranowski? What do you think made him so effective in leading others?

YOUR MISSION, YOUR IMPACT

We might not be living under a totalitarian regime, but we do live in a culture that is increasingly hostile to Christianity. Almost everywhere we turn, we are bombarded with a secular outlook on life: in the shows we watch, in the music we listen to, in our schools, in our workplaces, and with our peers. Who am I? Why am I here? What is love? What is marriage? What brings true happiness? Is there moral truth? Is there a God?

Many young people go to college without ever hearing the Gospel message or having the opportunity to be formed as a Christian disciple. Married couples don't get much support from the culture to live a Christian marriage. Parents struggle to raise kids in today's world, and parish leaders recognize that traditional methods of passing on the Faith aren't working in the new cultural situation. *Notes* Like Poland in the 1940s, the Church once again needs missionary disciples like Jan Tyranowski who will work against this cultural opposition, form others to live as disciples of Jesus, and train them to reach their peers with the Gospel.

That's why your mission to walk with others in discipleship is so important, and it comes with tremendous responsibility. The way you go about discipleship matters: how much prayer and planning you put into it; how well you form others in the Faith; how well you train them for mission. If done well, with the right vision and with great care, you, like Jan Tyranowski, can change the world. If that's going to happen, our discipleship with others must be intentional, like Jan's.

What made Jan Tyranowski's work in discipleship so powerful? He didn't just hang out with his men and get to know them. He certainly lived authentic friendship with them, but he did so with a purpose: to invite them to become missionary disciples themselves. He didn't just show up for meetings and shoot from the hip. He didn't just start another program. And he did a lot more than pray with his men, help them with their problems, and hold them accountable. He likely did some of that, but he also gave those he was leading an intentional formation in the Faith and equipped them to go out to reach others.

These articles will help you accomplish that same formation. The articles collected here are tools to help you form others to become missionary disciples. They'll help you maximize your time with others for greater impact. They'll provide more structure and depth to your investment in others while keeping things authentic and conversational. They'll give you a map as you bring others with you on the journey of "Win-Build-Send" (see Preface). By using these articles effectively, you too can help others experience a dynamic, transformative discipleship just like Venerable Jan Tyranowski.

Finally, we must remember that Jesus is the One who ultimately makes disciples, and he does this through his Church. Anyone we may be walking with in discipleship is technically not our own disciple, but a disciple of Jesus. Whether we are like Jan Tyranoski and find ourselves just a few steps ahead in life or one in a group of people striving to grow as Christian disciples, we are all on the journey of discipleship together and can encourage each other to grow in the imitation of Christ. It is our hope that these articles can equip you to lead others more effectively on this journey.

DISCUSS

In what ways has your experience in discipleship either resonated with or fallen short of the intentional discipleship of Venerable Jan Tyranowski? How might having discipleship resources like these help you give others more than what you could give them on your own?

DISCIPLESHIP AS CATHOLICS

It's important to note that these articles are not simply the result of individual creative opinions about discipleship or one organization's way of approaching evangelization. Rather, these articles are rooted in the Catholic Church's teachings on evangelization, catechesis, and discipleship. While there may be many other authentic expressions of missionary discipleship, these articles represent our attempt to live out and explain this Catholic vision for the process of leading people to a deeper encounter with Jesus Christ, to a more intentional walk with him as his disciples, and to inviting and equipping them to evangelize others. We simply seek to follow what the Church teaches about proclaiming the Gospel and forming missionary disciples. It is our hope that these articles will equip you to do this well within the heart of the Catholic Church.

We believe these articles will be a blessing for how you walk in discipleship with others in four main ways:

1. Your time in discipleship with others will be more **authentic and conversational**, allowing you to have natural conversations with others about important topics in a one-on-one or a group setting.

2. Your work in missionary discipleship will be more **repeatable**, equipping others not only to live as disciples themselves, but also to go out and form others to become effective missionary disciples as well.

3. You will take the people you lead **deeper** in their formation.

4. You will have great **flexibility** in your discipleship time.

HOW TO USE THE DISCIPLESHIP ARTICLES: 4 STEPS

These articles are designed to help you effectively lead others. As you plan to use these articles in your mission field, here are a few important steps to follow.

1. **Preparation: Read and pray through it on your own.** Take time to pray through the articles yourself so you can speak to others from your own experience and encounter with Christ. Also pray to better discern where people are in their walk with Christ, what they need, and what points you might want to emphasize to encourage them, inspire them or help them grow in a certain area.

2. **Master the stories and Key Concepts.** Each article includes "Key Concepts" you will want to reinforce in the conversation to ensure they are understood. These are important points that the person needs to grasp well, both for themselves and for the sake of others whom they might be called to journey with in discipleship down the road. So long as you communicate these main ideas, feel free to discuss the points in the article in a way that best meets your needs.

Notes

3. **Keep it personal: Use the article as a tool to build authentic conversations**.

   When you gather to discuss these articles, feel free to take turns reading the article aloud together and discussing the questions. As you discuss the article, keep your conversation personal and authentic by sharing your own experiences, stories, examples from saints, and examples of how these truths have personally impacted you. Feel free to add other questions or even depart from the article at times to let the conversation flow. Don't just ask the discussion questions to complete a task in a process. Rather, use those discussion questions or others you come up with to facilitate a conversation.

4. **Takeaways/Next Steps**.

   After discussing the article, talk together about what points inspired or challenged each of you the most. Share what you took away from the article and how you want to live these truths better. Ask the people you are working with what steps they might want to take to live out these truths in their own lives more intentionally. Remember, you are accompanying them on the journey of missionary discipleship. Use the article to start a process of transformation, but don't let it end there.

DISCUSS

How might these articles help you be more effective in your mission? What do you need to do to prepare to use these articles?

TAKE ACTION

Now that you understand what these articles are for and how to use them well, it's time to use them in your mission. Remember, these articles aren't primarily for you as the leader. This isn't simply a book that you read and reflect upon. These articles are tools that are meant to be used to help lead others in the Christian life and in mission.

For those of you already familiar with the idea of discipleship and forming others to become missionary disciples, it's time to start using these articles in your mission. Discern the needs of the people you serve and begin forming them in an intentional way using this tool.

For those of you who aren't as familiar with discipleship and how to walk with others in this way, consider taking some time to read a few of the later articles in this book for yourself, particularly the article "A Vision for Missionary Discipleship: 'Win-Build-Send'" on pg. 156. This article will give you an overview of the process of making missionary disciples.

Finally, the image on the following page shows you which articles are meant to be led at each of the various phases in someone's journey of discipleship. If you'd like more information on which articles to use with those whom you are serving, read the "For the Leader" section at the beginning of each main section. These will provide additional instructions regarding with whom you should use the articles in that section. That being said, be prudent in the way you use the articles and discern the needs of the people you are serving. Sometimes a later article might need to come earlier in the process, or vice versa, and that's okay. What's most important is that you form others well.

Take a few minutes to decide on some steps you can take to begin sharing these articles effectively.

DISCIPLESHIP ARTICLES

WIN
Accept the Gospel
(Jn 17:3)

BUILD

SEND
Accept the High Call to Mission
(Mt 28:18-20)

ENCOUNTER
1.0 Something More
1.1 God's Fatherly Love

THE GOSPEL
2.0 The Gospel

ACTS 2.42
3.0 "In the Dust of the Rabbi": Living as a Disciple of Jesus
3.1 Prayer: Spiritual Breathing
3.2 Fellowship: Virtuous Friendships
3.3 Sacraments: Eucharist
3.4 Sacraments: The Healing Power of Confession
3.5 The Apostles' Teaching: The Battle for Your Mind

THE HIGH CALL TO MISSION
4.0 Moral Authority and "The Big 3"
4.1 Faithfulness to Christ and His Church
4.2 The High Call to Mission

MISSION FORMATION
5.0 A Vision for Missionary Discipleship: Win-Build-Send
5.1 Incarnational Evangelization: The Art of Accompaniment
5.2 The Power of Your Testimony
5.3 Leading a Transformative Bible Study
5.4 Sharing the Gospel: A Call to Conversion
5.5 Walking With Others in Discipleship

PERSONAL FORMATION
6.0 Pursuing Christlike Character
6.1 Deeper Prayer: Persevering in Love
6.2 Works of Mercy
6.3 Intercessory Prayer
6.4 "Take Up Your Cross and Follow Me": Embracing the Cross in Mission

---

PROCESS OF EVANGELIZATION

"Above all the Gospel must be proclaimed by witness." — EN 21

"There is no true evangelization if the name, the teaching, the life, the promises, the kingdom and the mystery of Jesus of Nazareth, the Son of God, are not proclaimed." — EN 22

"Proclamation only reaches full development when it is listened to, accepted and assimilated, and when it arouses a genuine adherence in the one who has thus received it." — EN 23

"It is unthinkable that a person should accept the Word and give himself to the kingdom without becoming a person who bears witness to it and proclaims it in his turn." — EN 24

"A serious preparation is needed for all workers of evangelization." — EN 73

Notes

Notes

WIN

WIN

For the Leader

"Win" articles are designed to prepare someone for a deeper encounter with Christ and to receive the Gospel. They invite people to consider their need for God. You will find two different kinds of articles in this section: Encounter articles and the Gospel.

ENCOUNTER

Encounter articles are for anyone who has not yet made a firm commitment to the Gospel. This could be a Catholic or a Christian who has received baptism or confirmation, but who doesn't yet have a living relationship with Jesus. They may have been sacramentalized, perhaps even catechized, but they have not yet been evangelized. Or it could be someone who has different beliefs or doesn't believe in God at all. Either way, these articles are designed to help them take one step closer to a relationship with Christ and making friendship with him the center of their lives.

These articles are not designed to provide everything necessary to win someone to Jesus and the Gospel. They are simply about tilling the soil and introducing people to the person of Jesus Christ. At this stage, it's most important for you to invest deeply in others' lives, love them personally, and witness to the goodness and beauty of the Christian life: "above all the Gospel must be proclaimed by witness."[1]

THE GOSPEL

At the culmination of the Win stage, before moving to Build, it is essential that we explicitly share the Gospel and invite others to say "yes" to Jesus.[2] The work of evangelization does not reach its climax until we proclaim the Gospel: "There is no true evangelization if the name, the teaching, the life, the promises, the kingdom and the mystery of Jesus of Nazareth, the Son of God, are not proclaimed."[3] This article will help you proclaim the Gospel effectively. Once someone has said "yes" to the Gospel, they are more prepared to receive a deeper formation in the Christian life.

Notes

[1] Paul VI, *Evangelii Nuntiandi*, accessed May 25, 2020, Vatican.va, 21.

[2] John Paul II, *Catechesi Tradendae*, accessed May 25, 2020, Vatican.va, 20.

[3] Paul VI, *Evangelii Nuntiandi*, accessed May 25, 2020, Vatican.va, 22.

Notes

ENCOUNTER

SOMETHING
MORE

In 2005, Tom Brady won his third Super Bowl. Already known as one of the greatest quarterbacks of all time, he had achieved the goal of a lifetime — three times!

But in an interview afterward, Brady revealed something surprising. When asked about what he thought of all he had accomplished, he said this:

> Why do I have three Super Bowl rings, and still think there's something greater out there for me? I mean, maybe a lot of people would say, "Hey man, this is what is." I reached my goal, my dream, my life. Me, I think ... it's gotta be more than this. I mean this can't be what it's all cracked up to be. I mean I've done it. I'm 27. And what else is there for me? ... I wish I knew. I wish I knew. I mean I think that's part of me trying to go out and experience other things. I love playing football, and I love being a quarterback for this team, but, at the same time, I think there's a lot of other parts about me that I'm trying to find.[1]

Tom Brady's experience recalls the popular U2 song: "I still haven't found what I'm looking for." This is something we all can relate to. No matter what good things we might experience in life — a great group of friends, a successful final grade, a profitable work project, a spouse, a great movie, our team winning the championship, a hard-earned vacation — after a while, we discover that none of these things fully satisfy us. We still long for something more. Ultimately, everyone is looking for happiness that is deep and that lasts.

In the biblical passage we'll look at today, Jesus has a conversation with a woman from Samaria. As we witness their encounter, we'll discover Jesus' response to her desire (and ours) for something more.

--- **DISCUSS** ---

Have you ever achieved or received something you thought would satisfy you and found that it didn't? How did you respond?

GIVE ME A DRINK (JOHN 4:7–9)

The Gospel of John tells of a woman who, like many people today, was searching for something more in life. Let's read the start of that story in John 4:7–9:

> So he came to a city of Samaria, called Sychar, near the field that Jacob gave to his son Joseph. Jacob's well was there, and so Jesus, wearied as he was with his journey, sat down beside the well. It was about the sixth hour [noon].
>
> There came a woman of Samaria to draw water. Jesus said to her, "Give me a drink." For his disciples had gone away into the city to buy food. The Samaritan woman said to him, "How is it that you, a Jew, ask a drink of me, a woman of Samaria?" For Jews have no dealings with Samaritans.

DISCUSS

This biblical passage draws attention to Jesus talking to a woman of Samaria. Why do you think this is significant?

_____

The fact that Jesus spoke to this woman from Samaria would have been shocking in the first-century Jewish world. Jews and Samaritans did not get along. Imagine a big, ugly family feud, carried out over the course of dozens of generations and hundreds of years. The gist of the falling-out was this: The Samaritans and Jews both used to be part of the one Kingdom of Israel, but through civil war and exile, they were separated. As a result, they hated each other and tried not to interact with one another. Samaritans also intermarried with pagan nations and started worshiping pagan gods (2 Kgs 17:24–31). As a result, they were viewed with disdain by the Jews.

LIVING WATER (JOHN 4:10-15)

Let's continue the story in John 4:10–15:

> Jesus answered her, "If you knew the gift of God, and who it is that is saying to you, 'Give me a drink,' you would have asked him, and he would have given you living water." The woman said to him, "Sir, you have nothing to draw with, and the well is deep; where do you get that living water? Are you greater than our father Jacob, who gave us the well, and drank from it himself, and his sons, and his cattle?"
>
> Jesus said to her, "Everyone who drinks of this water will thirst again, but whoever drinks of the water that I shall give him will never thirst; the water that I shall give him will become in him a spring of water welling up to eternal life." The woman said to him, "Sir, give me this water, that I may not thirst, nor come here to draw."

—————————————— **DISCUSS** ——————————————

Both Jesus and the woman use the word "water," but they seem to be talking about two different kinds of water. What kind of water is the woman looking for? What do you think Jesus might be talking about when he speaks of "living water"?

Everyone who drinks of this water will thirst again, but whoever dinks of the water that I shall give him will never thirst.

—John 4:13-14

The woman is looking for water from the well — i.e., ordinary water for drinking. She is understandably puzzled about how Jesus could provide the water from the well since he has "nothing to draw with, and the well is deep" (Jn 4:11). She seems a bit suspicious of his claim to be able to provide her with water.

As the conversation moves on, however, she becomes more curious, intrigued that Jesus somehow might be able to provide her a never-ending water source. She says, "Sir, give me this water …" — but she still thinks of this water as merely drinking water from the well: "… that I may not thirst, nor come here to draw" (Jn 4:15).

In the Bible, water is a symbol of new life, spiritual life, and God coming to bring healing and forgiveness of sins. In Ezekiel 47, for example, waters pour out of the temple to bring life and healing to trees, fruit, and fish of every kind (Ez 47:7–12). In other passages, God himself is described as a fountain of living water (Jer 2:13; 17:13). When Jesus describes himself offering "living water," he's portraying himself as the living water of God: the water that brings life, healing, and forgiveness. Jesus is the one who quenches our deepest thirsts, which nothing in this world can fulfill — thirsts that ultimately are for God.

DISCUSS

Jesus is using the image of water to describe our deep human thirsts. What do you think people are thirsting for today? And what do people often turn toward to try to satisfy this thirst?

People today are thirsting for meaning and purpose. They long to be known. They yearn for acceptance, respect, friendship, and love. Ultimately, even if they don't realize it, they desire a happiness which can only be found in God.

To satisfy their thirsts, however, people try turning to things like success, wealth, status, or sex, which can never bring lasting happiness. They ignore the deeper longings of their hearts, distracting themselves with incessant noise, activity, busyness, and entertainment. They amuse themselves with social media, shows, and screens. They do everything they can to avoid being alone in the silence of their hearts and the stillness of their souls. But none of these approaches can satisfy the deepest thirsts of the human heart, which only leave us with emptiness, restlessness, and a yearning for something more. As St. Augustine once said, "You have made us for yourself, and our heart is restless until it rests in you."[2]

Notes

"I HAVE NO HUSBAND" (JOHN 4:16–19)

Read John 4:16–19:

> Jesus said to her, "Go, call your husband, and come here." The woman answered him, "I have no husband." Jesus said to her, "You are right in saying, 'I have no husband'; for you have had five husbands, and he whom you now have is not your husband; this you said truly." The woman said to him, "Sir, I perceive that you are a prophet."

DISCUSS

How has the woman been seeking to quench her deep thirst? How's that been going for her?

Like some people today, this particular woman has been seeking to fulfill her deepest desires, her thirsts, in a series of failed romantic relationships. Jesus already knows her heart-wrenching story of going from one man to the next; he also points out that the man she's with now is not truly committed to her either: "He whom you now have is not your husband" (Jn 4:18).

Having her life story told to her by Jesus, the woman starts to see something more in him. She realizes Jesus is no ordinary man. He is the prophet sent from God (Dt 18:15).

───────────────── **DISCUSS** ─────────────────

What do you think it's like to be this Samaritan woman? What do you think she's thinking at this moment in John's Gospel?

It's likely that this woman already was an outcast in her community. The fact that she comes to the well at "the sixth hour" (Jn 4:6) — which is noon, according to the ancient Jewish way of keeping time — is telling. This is not the normal time for women to be dragging their jugs to the well to fill them with water; that would normally be done in the early morning or evening when it was cooler. At those times, the women of the village would come together and socialize. The fact that this particular woman comes to the well at high noon, in the heat of the day, suggests that she has been ostracized by her community and that she is too ashamed to come out when others are there.

As a result, she probably felt very alone, forgotten, and abandoned. Then, think about how she might have felt to have Jesus bring her sad life out into the open. That might have only added to her feelings of embarrassment, guilt, shame, despair, and worthlessness.

But that's not what happens. Jesus doesn't condemn her. He wants to offer her a fresh start in life. He gently points out her misdirected desires and lovingly offers her a better way. His point is this: God is the only one who can fill our need for love, even though we often chase other things to fill this void. Jesus' encounter with the Samaritan woman symbolizes this dynamic. Jesus is revealed as the one who will fulfill the deepest thirst of our hearts: our thirst for God.

In the end, the woman seems to feel loved and cared for by Jesus. She perceives Jesus is the great prophet sent by God (Dt 18:15). And, as we will see next, she goes on to joyously tell others about Jesus.

LEAVING THE JAR BEHIND (JOHN 4:25–30)

Read John 4:25–30:

> The woman said to him, "I know that Messiah is coming (he who is called Christ); when he comes, he will show us all things." Jesus said to her, "I who speak to you am he."
>
> Just then his disciples came. They marveled that he was talking with a woman, but none said, "What do you wish?" or, "Why are you talking with her?" So the woman left her water jar, and went away into the city, and said to the people, "Come, see a man who told me all that I ever did. Can this be the Christ?"

Christians throughout the centuries have seen profound symbolism in the woman leaving her jar behind. She came to the well with her jar, hoping to fill it with water from the well. She leaves the well with something so much greater, having encountered Jesus Christ, the living water who fulfills our deepest thirsts. Leaving her jar behind symbolizes that she is giving up her old life and her pursuit of earthly things to fulfill her heart's desires.

––––––––––––––––––––––– **DISCUSS** –––––––––––––––––––––––

Put yourself in the shoes of the Samaritan woman. What "water jugs" do you think God wants you to leave behind to make more room for those things which truly satisfy?

For additional insights into this passage, see the "Additional Background" Supplemental Resource on the next page.

SUPPLEMENTAL RESOURCE:

1.0 SOMETHING MORE

ADDITIONAL BACKGROUND

Symbolism of the Well (Jn 4:7–9)

In the Bible, the well is a place where many of Israel's ancient leaders found their wives: Isaac's wife Rebecca (Gn 24:11); Jacob's wife Rachel (Gn 29:2) and Moses' wife Zipporah (Ex 2:15). Now Jesus meets a Samaritan woman at the well. However, instead of marriage as we usually think of it, Jesus is setting the stage for a relationship with him that is even more profound.

Symbolism of the Five Husbands (Jn 4:16–19)

The fact that the woman has been married to five men is very significant.

The Samaritans intermarried with five foreign nations. These nations introduced their own gods; the main one was Baal, which, in Hebrew, can mean "lord" or even "husband." When the Samaritans intermarried, they also accepted these foreign gods of the pagan nations around them, spurning their relationship with the one true God himself, their true husband.

Throughout the Old Testament, when the Israelites worship foreign gods, it is considered an act of covenant infidelity. The prophets even compared it to adultery. This was a fitting description because "God's relationship with Israel was likened to the kind of intimate union that exists between a husband and a wife: God was the bridegroom and Israel was the Bride. The Samaritans' unfaithfulness to the covenant and their worshiping of other gods was, according to the prophets, similar to the infidelity of a spouse."[3]

But the prophets foretold that, one day, God would come back to Samaria as a bridegroom. Despite Samaria's infidelities, the Lord, the divine bridegroom, would come to his spouse again, speak to her in love, and call her back into relationship. God foretold this in the Book of Hosea: "I will allure her, and bring her into the wilderness, and speak tenderly to her … For I will remove the names of the Ba'als from her mouth, and they shall be mentioned no more. And I will make for you a covenant … And I will betroth you to me forever" (Hos 2:14, 17–20).

Now, centuries later, Jesus comes to this woman of Samaria and fulfills this prophecy. He is the divine bridegroom coming to reunite the Samaritan people to himself. Two facts support this: First, Jesus is explicitly called the "bridegroom" by John the Baptist (Jn 3:29–30). Second, Jesus meets her at a well, which in Scripture has important marital symbolism. Now Jesus, who already is called the "bridegroom," meets a Samaritan woman not in any ordinary location but specifically *at a well*.

> As we listen to their conversation, we discover that the Samaritan woman has had a heart-wrenching life — one that actually embodies the disastrous history of her nation. She has suffered through the misery of marital infidelity. Like Samaria, she had been an adulterous wife; she yoked herself to five different men, just as Samaria had yoked itself to five foreign nations and their idolatrous practices (2 Kgs 17:29–34). Her life, therefore, is an icon of the covenant infidelity of Israel that Hosea had condemned.
>
> But now, Jesus tenderly approaches her as the divine bridegroom seeking out unfaithful Samaria to woo her back into covenant union, just as Hosea prophesied. He speaks gently to her and extends his loving mercy. As the ever-faithful husband, Jesus does not reject her but invites her to return to God's kingdom.[4]

God's point is this: He is the only one who can fill our need for love, yet we continue to chase other things to fill this void. Jesus and the Samaritan woman symbolize this dynamic. Jesus comes as the true husband to this Samaritan woman, the Samaritan people — and the world.

Notes

[1] Tom Brady, "Transcript: Tom Brady, Part 3," interview by Steve Kroft, *60 Minutes*. November 4, 2005. https://www.cbsnews.com/news/transcript-tom-brady-part-3/.

[2] Augustine, *Confessions*, trans. John K. Ryan (New York: Image, 1960), I.i.1.

[3] Curtis Martin and Edward Sri, *The Real Story: Understanding the Big Picture of the Bible* (Hebron, KY: Dynamic Catholic, 2012), 139.

[4] Ibid., 141 – 42.

GOD'S FATHERLY LOVE

E dward Zwick's 2006 film *Blood Diamond* presents the story of the reunion of a father and his child.

The story is gruesome: Set in Sierra Leone in 1999, the movie begins with rebel factions terrorizing the countryside, intimidating locals and enslaving some to mine diamonds. One such unfortunate local is a young fisherman, Solomon Vandy.

Solomon escapes the mining camp only to find that his son, Dia, has been captured by revolutionary forces and is now being forced to serve as a child soldier. Solomon's heart is wrecked. He had been a good father his entire life: raising his family in love, coaching his son in soccer, and participating in the life of the African Mendy tribe. He loves his son more than anything, and he knows how much Dia must be suffering.

The life of a child soldier is horrific. Desperate from poverty, traumatized by war and crazed for diamonds, many child soldiers turn to drugs, alcohol, and sexual debauchery to numb the pain. Dia is no different. He needs an escape, and pleasure brings a welcome distraction. Dia's life has become a mixture of depressing work and passing pleasure, very different from the life he knew with his father as a young boy. At first, Dia hoped his father would come. But soon, as the days turn to weeks, Dia's apathy increases and he lets his trust in his father slip away. Eventually Dia becomes seriously depressed and even resents Solomon for failing to rescue him from his misery.

One day, everything changes. Bullets break the morning calm of the rebel encampment. A rival force has come to save the day, and among them is Dia's father, Solomon. Finally, father and son will be reunited — but just as things seem to come to a resolution, a new crisis ensues.

Solomon runs to Dia and tries to embrace him, but much to Solomon's surprise, Dia refuses to acknowledge his father. Brainwashed by the rebel army, Dia thinks to himself, "I can barely remember the life I knew with my family, and I have done so many bad things. How could I ever return?"

Solomon comes closer, but Dia will not relent. Scared that he might lose his pleasure, money, and power, Dia grabs a nearby gun and points it directly at his father.

But Solomon is not afraid. Instead, returning his son's gaze, he says, "Dia! What are you doing? Dia, look at me!"

Now, peering over the sight of his gun, Dia feels a lump in his throat as his father's dark eyes look directly into his soul. These are the same eyes that looked at Dia as a baby. The same eyes that watched Dia play soccer. The same eyes that shone with laughter at family dinners with Dia. These were the eyes of Dia's father, a loving father, a father who yearned for Dia to come to his senses. But Dia could not do it, and though tears streamed down his face, he continued to squeeze the trigger.

Dia's father remains firm. He walks towards Dia with tears in his eyes, reminding Dia of his identity, his home, where he came from: "You are Dia Vandy of the proud Mendy tribe. You are a good boy who loves soccer and school."

Dia's hands begin to sweat; his chest quivers and tears run down his cheeks.

His father continues, *"Dia, I know they made you do bad things, but you are not a bad boy. I am your father, who loves you, and you will come home with me and be my son again."*

At this, Dia breaks. Lowering his gun, he allows himself, in his heart, to return to the identity he'd once known. He allows himself, once again, to trust his father, and his father comes and embraces him.[1]

—————————————————— **DISCUSS** —————————————————— *Notes*

Why was it difficult for Dia to accept the love of his father? What do you think allowed Dia to return to his father?

A NEW LOOK AT THE PRODIGAL SON

The movie *Blood Diamond* won awards at multiple film festivals, and Djimon Hounsou (Solomon Vandy) was nominated for an Oscar. His portrayal of a good father inspired the hearts of millions of viewers. One reason for the movie's success is that it speaks to a universal human desire: the desire for love, for acceptance, for healing, and for true fatherhood. But more than anything else, and particularly in this scene, the movie is about *identity*. The movie is about a son who remembers his own identity and that of his father's. At the turning point, when Dia lowers the gun, it's almost as if he thinks to himself, "Oh yes, I remember you: my father, the man I knew before the war. And I remember who I am: your son."

Man's search for identity lies at the core of the human experience. Solomon reminded Dia of his identity as a son and tribe member, but many of us in this present world do not have anyone to tell us our identity. We walk through life with questions, but no answers. We don't know who we are, and we don't know who God is. But we want to know, and it is these two questions which, in the end, motivate all other religious questions: God, who are you? And who am I?

There are a variety of competing offers to address these questions. One answer is *atheism*, the belief that there is no God and you ultimately have no significant identity save perhaps the identity of a random speck in an insignificant universe. Another answer is *deism*, the idea that there is a God, but he is not involved in your daily life. Yet another answer is that God is an all-powerful slave-

driver or a disconnected judge. None of these false views is the God of Christianity. The Christian view of God is different from all other religions in the world. It not only gives us an answer to our two questions — *Who is God?* and *Who am I?* — but it also tells us something about why we are so enraptured by stories like Solomon and Dia.

How so? Well, the Bible contains a story much like Dia's story. Of the many parables Jesus told, the most famous is called the Parable of the Prodigal Son from the Gospel of Luke. Why is this one the most beloved? You may have heard this parable before, but before you write it off as cliché, ask yourself: Why has this parable inspired the hearts and minds of billions of people? Let's take a look:

> And [Jesus] said, "There was a man who had two sons; and the younger of them said to his father, 'Father, give me the share of property that falls to me.' And he divided his living between them. Not many days later, the younger son gathered all he had and took his journey into a far country, and there he squandered his property in loose living. And when he had spent everything, a great famine arose in that country, and he began to be in want. So he went and joined himself to one of the citizens of that country, who sent him into his fields to feed swine. And he would gladly have fed on the pods that the swine ate; and no one gave him anything. But when he came to himself he said, 'How

many of my father's hired servants have bread enough *Notes*
and to spare, but I perish here with hunger! I will arise and
go to my father, and I will say to him, "Father, I have sinned
against heaven and before you; I am no longer worthy to
be called your son; treat me as one of your hired servants.'"
(Lk 15:11–19)

─────────────────────── **DISCUSS** ───────────────────────

Why do you think the son left his father, and why does he think
about coming back? How do you think the son views himself in
this moment?

───

TRUST

The experience of the prodigal son is so typical of almost any
human story. Let's review the basic narrative thus far: The prodigal
son sinned against his father, felt ashamed and then felt unworthy
of the father's love. In short, the prodigal son's actions caused him
to doubt his father's love. This tendency to doubt fatherly love,
especially God's love, is a typical part of the human experience.

The prodigal son thinks of his father more like a master and himself
as a slave. He doesn't feel like he can have a relationship with his
father. He's failed miserably, and he knows it. His choices have
consequences. He starts thinking back to his father, but he assumes
things can never be the same. He's ruined it. He'll just have to be a
slave, a cog in the wheel of his father's unforgiving universe. He sees
his actions as his identity — thinking, for example, "I'm not good
enough. In fact, I am worthless, and I don't deserve real love."

The story of the prodigal son has universal appeal because it
highlights a universal cycle: temptation, then sin, then shame, then
isolation. Paradoxically, before the cycle begins, people often think

sin is not a big deal. Yet, after the cycle ends, people think their sin is such a big deal that they have no route back to God!

DISCUSS

Can you relate to the story of the prodigal son? Have you ever lost trust in God, or have you ever felt like you couldn't go back to God? Have you ever experienced this reality on a human level with someone else in your life?

COMING HOME

Most of us can relate to the prodigal son, so let's see how the story ends:

> "And he arose and came to his father. But while he was yet at a distance, his father saw him and had compassion, and ran and embraced him and kissed him. And the son said to him, 'Father, I have sinned against heaven and before you; I am no longer worthy to be called your son.' But the father said to his servants, 'Bring quickly the best robe, and put it on him; and put a ring on his hand, and shoes on his feet; and bring the fatted calf and kill it, and let us eat and make merry; for this my son was dead, and is alive again; he was lost, and is found.'" (Lk 15:20–24)

While he was still a long way off, his father caught sight of him, and was filled with compassion.
—Luke 15:20

Contrary to what the prodigal son expected, his father refuses to treat him as a slave. In fact, the father celebrates his return. His father has been watching from a distance, eagerly awaiting his son's homecoming. The fact that his son has even started his return journey is enough to send the father running to meet him. The son begins explaining his actions, but for the father, the mere fact that the son is interested in coming home is enough to throw a party! The robe and the ring reveal that the son is fully restored. The son

Notes

comes back feeling like a slave, but the father insists that he live as his son.

You might ask, what does all this have to do with our original two questions: *God, who are you? And who am I?* The Parable of the Prodigal Son gives us Christianity's answer. Who is God? He is an all-loving father *(Catechism of the Catholic Church* 238–40).[2] Who are you? You are his child. Scripture is clear that the Lord of the universe, the infinite God and the only being capable of satisfying our desires, is a good father. Christianity is utterly unique among world religions in this radical claim: God is a good Father. He is not a slave driver. He is not out to get you. Nothing you have done can separate you from his love. Your identity has nothing to do with anything that you've done. Indeed, God thirsts for you. Just like Solomon Vandy and the prodigal son's father, he longs for you, and you have infinite value in his eyes.

In the end, Christianity gives a clear answer to who you are: God is father, and your identity lies in the fact that you are God's son or daughter! That is who you are!

Having trouble believing this? Perhaps, like Dia, the wars of your own life have you pointing a gun at God. Or perhaps, like the prodigal son, you think something you've done means you can't go back to God. But nothing could be further from the truth. Like Dia, allow God to remind you of your identity. Like the prodigal son, take the first step back home. Return, lower the gun, allow God the chance to show you his love. Allow yourself to once again — or perhaps for the first time — begin a relationship with him.

DISCUSS

How do you think God sees you right now? What do you think about when you consider coming closer (or returning) to God? Do you believe that God is your loving Father?

Notes

Notes

[1] *Blood Diamond,* directed by Edward Zwick (2006; California: Warner Bros, 2007), DVD.

[2] "By calling God 'Father,' the language of faith indicates two main things: that God is the first origin of everything and transcendent authority; and that he is at the same time goodness and loving care for all his children." (CCC 239)

THE GOSPEL

2.0

THE
GOSPEL

"A s Jesus passed on from there, he saw a man called Matthew sitting at the tax office; and he said to him, 'Follow me.' And he rose and followed him" (Mt 9:9).

Consider Matthew the tax collector. Collecting taxes wasn't simply another profession in the time of Jesus. Tax collectors were responsible for extracting money from people, and they often did so without mercy. They stole from the people, increasing tax rates and pocketing the extra money for themselves.

As a *Jewish* tax collector, Matthew would have been viewed as even worse. Roman rule was a serious problem for the Jews. God had given them the Promised Land, and they were supposed to have their own king, not a Roman emperor. Rome was the enemy, and anyone who stood with Rome was an outcast, a friend of the enemy. That's Matthew.

Matthew is a thief. He's a traitor. He's given in to the allure of wealth and of power. When Jesus says to Matthew, "Follow me," you can imagine the conflict in Matthew's mind: "Can I really give it up? What about my money, my career?" Yet, at the same time, he longs for something more in life: "Would I be happier? Would life be better if I left everything and followed this man? Maybe I don't have to be a traitor. But can I really change? Do I even *want* to change? Do I even know this man? What happens if I follow him? What's it going to cost?"

Jesus' invitation to "follow me" is one that he offers to each of us. And like Matthew, we might feel the tension. Maybe we've been there before. Maybe we're not sure following Jesus is a good decision. Maybe we sense God calling us to something, but we're afraid of what it might cost. Maybe we've done some bad things in the past and don't think we can change. Whatever our situation, let's consider Jesus' invitation to "follow me" and see what it might mean for our lives.

DISCUSS

Like Matthew, have you ever felt this conflict in your life? How so?

AN INVITATION: FIVE Rs

Jesus' invitation can be summarized by 5 Rs: Relationship, Rebellion, Reconciliation, Re-Creation, and Response. Let's look at this message and discover what it might mean for us.

As you get started, consider this question:

———————————————— DISCUSS ————————————————

What do you think life is all about?

RELATIONSHIP: WHAT WE'RE MADE FOR

Throughout human history, many answers to the question of the meaning of life have been proposed. But the Christian answer to this question is unique: "God, infinitely perfect and blessed in himself, in a plan of sheer goodness freely created man to make him share in his own blessed life" (CCC 1). Think about that: God did not have any *need* to create us — he is perfectly blessed in himself. Yet, as the Bible teaches, "God is love" (1 Jn 4:8), and out of love, he freely chose to bring us into existence and fill us with his life, so that he could share his love with us. This is where we find enduring, lasting happiness: in friendship with God as his sons and daughters (Gn 1:26).

———————————————— DISCUSS ————————————————

What do you think of the Christian answer to the meaning of life? Do you think you can have a relationship with God?

REBELLION: THE CHASM

Though we are made for a relationship with God, there is a serious problem: sin.

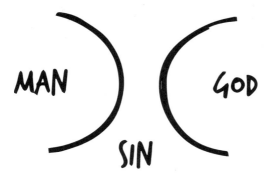

Sin radically ruptures our relationship with God. We must feel the weight of how devastating the consequences of sin are. As Curtis Martin explains in his book *Making Missionary Disciples*,

> You are not who you were meant to be. Sin wounded you and separated you from God. Our problem is actually far worse than we might have imagined. At first glance, we may think that, with some effort toward self-improvement, we could close the gap between who we are and who we ought to be. It is simply not the case.
>
> When we fell: The fall was *universal* — "All have sinned and fall short of the glory of God" (Rom 3:23).
>
> The fall was *severe* — "For the wages of sin is death" (Rom 6:23).[1]

God, infinitely perfect and blessed in himself, in a plan of sheer goodness freely created man to make him share in his own blessed life.

— Catechism of the Catholic Church 1

The fall created a chasm so great that no human could bridge it, not even with their best effort. The problem of our lives is not primarily found in our circumstances — our family, our boyfriend or girlfriend, the political situation we find ourselves in, our job, or anything else that has happened to us. Our problem is sin.

Sin leads to a dilemma: We are made for a relationship with God, yet we are separated from him because of sin. And despite our best efforts, we can't bridge the gap caused by sin.

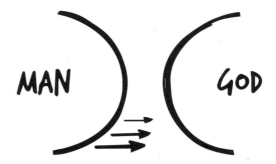

Think of what happens in other relationships. When we hurt someone, we have a sense that we should do something — offer a gift of love, a sacrifice, an expression of our sorrow and desire to set things right — so that we can bridge the gap in the relationship. The same is true in our relationship with God. But with God, the gift of love, the bridge, must be so much greater, infinitely greater. As Dr. Edward Sri explains in his book *Love Unveiled,*

> Our sin entails withholding our love for the God who so completely loves us. We, therefore, should offer God a gift of love that corresponds to the infinite gravity of sin committed against him. But no human being can do that. Not even the most saintly person could offer a gift of love that would atone for the sins of all humanity. Only a divine person could do that.[2]

This is the dilemma. We have a desire for a lasting happiness that only comes from a relationship with God, but we are unable to amend that relationship ourselves. We are finite, and only an infinite love can bridge the infinite gap caused by sin.

DISCUSS

How have you experienced sin and its effects? How have you experienced this dilemma? In what ways have you tried to "get right with God" on your own, either directly or indirectly?

Notes

RECONCILIATION: THE GOD-MAN SOLUTION

So, how can this dilemma be solved? The only way is the God-man solution: Jesus Christ. As God and man, only Jesus Christ can bridge the infinite gap between us and God.

- *As fully human*, Jesus can represent us. He can offer an act of love on behalf of the entire human family.

- But because he is also *fully divine*, Jesus' act of love far surpasses anything a mere human could ever offer.

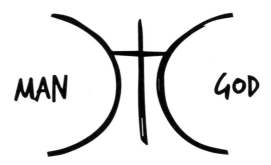

Because of who Jesus is, fully human and fully divine, his total, self-giving love on the cross takes on infinite value. As the God-man, Jesus offers on our behalf an infinite gift of love that restores us to right relationship with the Father. Jesus is the bridge between sinful humanity and the all-holy God.

What do you think of the idea of Jesus giving his life for you? Do you believe that Jesus' sacrifice on the cross can redeem the damage done by sin?

RE-CREATION: TRANSFORMATION IN CHRIST

But there's more. Jesus came to do a lot more than die on the cross for our sins. If all Jesus did was die on the cross, humanity would have made amends with God, things would be repaired and a right relationship with the Father would be restored. But God loves us so much that he wants so much more than merely a repaired, just, peaceful coexisting relationship with us. He wants our hearts. He wants to make us a "new creation"[3] (2 Cor 5:17).

Curtis Martin explains an image that the Church Fathers gave us for the profound transformation in Christ that God wants to work in our lives:

> Imagine a cold steel bar and a hot burning fire. They have almost nothing in common. If you place the cold rod in the hot fire, though, something amazing begins to happen: the rod begins to take on the properties of the fire. It grows warm, it begins to glow — and if you were to take the rod out of the fire and touch it to some straw, it could actually start a fire itself. Now imagine that the fire is God and we are the steel rod. When we are living in Christ ... we begin to take on the properties of God.[4]

This is so much more than merely being forgiven of our sins! As Christ fills us with his life, we begin to think like Christ, serve like Christ, sacrifice like Christ. We take on the qualities of Christ. We become more patient, honest, generous, pure, and courageous

Take, Lord, and receive all my liberty, my memory, my understanding, and my entire will, all that I have and possess.

— St. Ignatius of Loyola

like Christ. As St. Paul explains, we are being changed into Christ's likeness from one degree of glory to another (2 Cor 3:18).

Christianity is not simply a self-help religion, a good way to be a nice person. Nor is it simply about being pardoned by a benevolent deity. At its root, Christianity is about allowing God to change us from within. We recognize our sinfulness and complete helplessness, and we allow God to forgive us, heal us and transform us — so that we can live and love like Christ himself. Jesus has not only died to offer us forgiveness; he has also risen to fill us with his life so that we can be transformed in him.

This transformation takes place in Christ's Church. It's through the Church that we truly encounter the living Jesus today and are changed. All that Jesus won for us in his death and resurrection comes to us through the Church, through its teachings and its sacraments. First, the teachings: The Catholic Church hands on the teachings of Christ so that we can be guided by him as our Lord. When we hear the teachings of the Church, we are encountering Christ speaking to us today. Second, the sacraments: The same Jesus who healed the sick, gave sight to the blind, and forgave people of their sins continues to touch our lives today through his *sacraments*. In the sacraments, we encounter the living Jesus who heals us of our own weaknesses, forgives us of our sins, and fills us with His Spirit so that our hearts can be made more like his. We encounter Jesus Christ himself in the Catholic Church. It is there that we are invited to follow him and are changed.

—————————————— **DISCUSS** ——————————————

Do you believe that God can bring about this kind of transformation in your life? What do you think about the idea that God wants to share his life with you and transform you in a specific way through the Church?

RESPONSE: "FOLLOW ME"

Jesus provides an answer that bridges the gap made by sin. Salvation is a gift, freely offered to each of us by God through the Church. The decision to say yes to God's saving gift means making the fundamental choice to become a disciple of Jesus (i.e. "Follow me"). God's gift is a complete gift of himself to us and for us; the only appropriate response is a complete gift of ourselves in return.

But, like Matthew in the Gospel story above, we can be hesitant. We have questions. We worry about what it might cost. But Jesus doesn't take away anything that makes life good:

> If we let Christ enter fully into our lives, if we open ourselves totally to him, are we not afraid that He might take something away from us? Are we not perhaps afraid to give up something significant, something unique, something that makes life so beautiful? ... No! If we let Christ into our lives, we lose nothing, nothing, absolutely nothing of what makes life free, beautiful and great ... Do not be afraid of Christ! He takes nothing away, and he gives you everything. When we give ourselves to him, we receive a hundredfold in return. Yes, open, open wide the doors to Christ — and you will find true life.[5]

As you consider Jesus' invitation, one way to think about your relationship with God is in three simple scenarios (illustrated by the images below):

  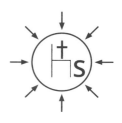

1	2	3

| God is not a part of my life. I rule over my life myself. | God is a part of my life, but he is not at the center. He's important and I involve him in my decisions sometimes, but I still rule over my life myself. | God is the very center of my life. I surrender my life, my plans and my dreams in his hands, and I seek to do his will and not my own. He is the Lord of my life. He is sitting on the throne of my heart. |

DISCUSS

1. *Looking at these three images, where would you place yourself? Why?*

2. *Right now, will you make the decision to place Jesus Christ at the center of your life? Will you give your life to him and choose to follow him?*

3. *(a) If not, what is preventing you from committing your life to Jesus as a disciple?*

   OR

   (b) If yes, will you pray right now to express your desire to invite Christ more deeply into your life?

Pray together in your own way, or use one of the following prayers from the tradition of the Church:

Notes

- *"Lord Jesus Christ, Son of God, have mercy on me, a sinner" (CCC 435).*

- *"Take, Lord, and receive all my liberty, my memory, my understanding, and my entire will, all that I have and possess. You have given all to me. To you, O Lord, I return it. All is Yours, dispose of it wholly according to Your will. Give me Your love and Your grace, for this is enough for me" (St. Ignatius of Loyola).*

TAKE ACTION

—————————— **DISCUSS** ——————————

What steps do you need to take to respond to Christ's invitation? What in your life needs to change? What practical steps do you need to take? See examples below:

- Going to confession

- Beginning to pray daily

- Going to Sunday (or even daily) Mass

- Reading Scripture daily

- Spending time with other Christians

- Joining RCIA

Notes

Notes

[1] Curtis Martin, *Making Missionary Disciples: How to Live the Method Modeled by the Master* (Colorado: FOCUS, 2018), 46-47.

[2] Edward Sri, *Love Unveiled: The Catholic Faith Explained* (San Francisco: Ignatius), 91.

[3] Pontifical Council for Culture, "Concluding Document of the Plenary Assembly: The *Via Pulcritudinous*, Priviliged Pathway for Evangelization and Dialogue (2006), accessed November 17, 2020, Vatican.va, III.1.

[4] Curtis Martin, *Making Missionary Disciples: How to Live the Method Modeled by the Master* (Colorado: FOCUS, 2018), 13.

[5] Benedict XVI, "Homily of his Holiness Benedict XVI, Imposition of the Pallium and Conferral of the Fisherman's Ring for the Beginning of the Petrine Ministry of the Bishop of Rome (April 2005)," accessed March 13, 2020, Vatican.va.

BUILD

BUILD
For the Leader

"Build" articles are designed to help those who have accepted the Gospel to continue to develop their relationship with Christ. Once someone has said yes to Jesus,[1] it's time to instruct them in the basic practices of the Catholic faith. According to Pope St. Paul VI, "proclamation only reaches full development when it is listened to, accepted, and assimilated, and when it arouses a genuine adherence in the one who has thus received it. An adherence to the truths which the Lord in his mercy has revealed; still more, an adherence to a program of life — a life henceforth transformed."[2] While the process of this assimilation and ongoing conversion lasts a lifetime, it's important to help disciples of Jesus begin cultivating a "program of life."[3]

ACTS 2:42

The articles in this section are not intended to offer a comprehensive catechesis. They are just a starting point, introducing the basics of what it means to be a disciple and the four foundational areas of the Christian life to which the earliest disciples devoted themselves: prayer, fellowship, the sacraments, and the teachings of the apostles (Acts 2:42). As you are forming others in these four areas, it is important that you are also *living* these things alongside them in a variety of ways — inviting them into the habits you have established in your own life and challenging them to make the habits their own.

THE HIGH CALL TO MISSION

At the culmination of the Build phase is the High Call to Mission. This is an explicit invitation to accept the mission of evangelization.

According to Paul VI, "it is unthinkable that someone should accept the Word and give himself to the kingdom without becoming a person who bears witness to it and proclaims it in his turn."[4] Articles in this section prepare faithful disciples of Jesus to understand and participate more fully in the Church's mission of evangelization and to accept the call to mission.

Notes

Notes

[1] John Paul II, *Catechesi Tradendae*, accessed May 25, 2020, Vatican.va, 20.

[2] Paul VI, *Evangelii Nuntiandi*, accessed May 25, 2020, Vatican.va, 23.

[3] Ibid.

[4] Ibid, 24.

Notes

ACTS 2:42

"IN THE DUST OF THE RABBI"

LIVING AS A DISCIPLE OF JESUS

Optional *Lectio Divina* Prayer

1. Read Luke 5:1–11.
2. Meditate on the words.
3. Speak to Christ about this passage.
4. Rest and listen in God's presence.
5. Discuss together.

It's astonishing that, of the thousands of Jewish people living in his day, Jesus chose a man like Simon Peter to be his disciple.

Peter did not come with an impressive résumé. He did not stand out as one of the smartest or holiest or most gifted or most talented people of his time, nor did he hold any position of leadership among the Jews. He was not a priest. He wasn't part of the elite ruling class. He wasn't a religious expert like the Pharisees. He was just an ordinary, uneducated fisherman working on the shores of the Sea of Galilee.

And it's clear from the Gospels that Peter was far from perfect. He does exhibit some moments of great faith, but he's also known for making big mistakes and overestimating his abilities, like misunderstanding Jesus (Mt 16:22), limiting forgiveness (Mt 18:21), and lacking in trust (Mt 14:30). Peter even denies Jesus three times and abandons him in his greatest hour of need (Mt 26:75).

Peter was an ordinary person like us — someone who had good intentions but didn't have it all together — and yet, Jesus still called him to be his disciple. And Peter's life was transformed through this process of discipleship: He eventually became a great Christian leader, a holy saint, a courageous witness to Christ, and even a martyr in Rome.

That gives us great encouragement. God loves and chooses us just as we are, but he loves us too much to let us stay there. It's the call to follow him that comes first, before the expectation to do great things. And if we answer the call, he will heal us and equip us to live as his disciples. If Jesus can take weak, imperfect, far-from-holy men like Peter and transform them over time into saints, he certainly can do the same with us.

—————————— DISCUSS ——————————

Does knowing that Peter was not necessarily the most gifted and talented person in the world encourage you? In what ways have you had good intentions to be who Jesus was calling you to be, but failed?

DISCIPLES OF JESUS: IMITATING THE MASTER[1]

The idea of discipleship can be summed up with one biblical key word: *imitation.* To be a disciple meant you were following a rabbi, a teacher. But the goal of a disciple wasn't merely to master the rabbi's teachings; instead, it was to master his way of life: how he prayed, studied, taught, served the poor, and lived out his relationship with God day to day.

Jesus himself said that, when a disciple is fully trained, he becomes "like his teacher" (Lk 6:40). When St. Paul formed disciples, he exhorted them not just to remember his teachings but also to follow his way of living: "Be imitators of me as I am of Christ" (1 Cor 11:1). He exhorted them to lead others in the same way (2 Tm 2:2).

The word the Bible uses for "disciple" is *mathetes*, which means "learner." But biblical discipleship is very different from the kind of classroom learning that takes place on most college campuses today. A university professor might deliver lectures in a large hall, and students would later be tested on how well they mastered the material they received. Occasionally, a student might ask a question and seek more guidance. But for the most part, professors and students usually don't share life together in an ongoing community of fellowship and learning outside the classroom.

Learning from a rabbi, however, was very different. As Edward Sri explains,

> To follow a rabbi ... meant living with the rabbi, sharing life with him and taking part in the rabbi's whole way of life. A disciple might accompany a rabbi on all his daily routines: prayer, study, debating other rabbis, giving alms to the poor, burying the dead, going to court, etc. A rabbi's life was meant to be a living example of someone shaped by God's Word. Disciples, therefore, studied not just the text of Scripture but also the "text" of the rabbi's life.[2]

This is why Jesus didn't simply invite his disciples to listen to his preaching in the synagogues. He said, "Come, follow me," and basically invited them on a three-year camping trip, traveling from village to village throughout Galilee as he was preaching the Gospel of the kingdom.

Think about that: living with Jesus, day in and day out, for three years! How much his disciples would have been influenced by his example! They'd notice the way he woke up early to pray. They'd witness his compassion toward others. They'd be moved by his urgent need to go out to sinners and outcasts. They'd see miracles of healing and resurrection. They'd also witness how he taught the crowds, debated opponents, called people to repentance and offered them his mercy. Much of Jesus' way of living would have "rubbed off" on his disciples.

How does this idea of discipleship change the way you think about what it means to be a disciple of Jesus?

OUR DISCIPLESHIP TODAY

While we're called to follow all the doctrines and practices of the Faith, much more is needed. We must go deeper and reflect upon what is happening in our hearts. Are we growing in our union with Jesus? Do we notice his ongoing call to conversion, his prompting in us to give more, love more, and surrender more? Disciples are aware that Jesus is constantly inviting them to live more like him in all areas of their lives — as Pope St. John Paul II said, "to think like him, to judge like him, to act in conformity with his commandments, and to hope as he invites us to."[4] Being a disciple, therefore, entails a lot more than simply saying and believing the right things. It's an entire way of life. It's ultimately Jesus' way of life transforming us.

This theme of discipleship reminds us that being Catholic is not something stagnant: "I attend Mass on Sundays"; "I believe all the Church's teachings." All that, of course, is essential for a practicing Catholic; but living as a disciple involves so much more. Discipleship is something intensely personal and dynamic. It entails ongoing conversion, transformation, and continually learning to say a greater "Yes" to Jesus. The true disciple of Jesus is never just going through the motions. They never settle for mediocrity, for the bare minimum, for a "check-the-box" approach to faith. Rather, true disciples are striving for greatness, always on the lookout for the next step of faith to which God is calling them. They are intentionally aiming to root out sins and weaknesses in their life, to grow in new virtues and to deepen their friendship with Christ. They're intentionally trying to imitate Christ.

This journey of transformation involves a disciple humbly recognizing two important truths:

A. **"The truth about himself**—his many weaknesses, failures, and areas where he falls short of living like Christ

B. **The truth about what he's made for**—being conformed to the image of Christ: living like him, loving like him ...

Discipleship is all about moving from A to B."[5]

When the Catholic tradition speaks about "pursuing sanctity" or "becoming holy," it's referring to this lifelong process of a Christian disciple being ever more transformed by God's grace and changed into Christ's likeness "from one degree of glory to another" (2 Cor 3:18).

--------------------- **DISCUSS** ---------------------

In what ways are you already living as a disciple of Jesus, and in what ways do you see yourself falling short?

LIVING AS A DISCIPLE: FOUR PRACTICES

The ancient Jews had a saying that captures this idea of discipleship and transformation. They said that if you find a good rabbi, you should "cover yourself in the dust of his feet and drink in his words thirstily." Sri goes on to explain:

> The expression probably draws on a well-known sight for ancient Jews: disciples were known for walking behind their rabbi, following him so closely that they would become covered with the dust kicked up from his sandals. This would have been a powerful image for what should happen in the disciple's life spiritually. Disciples were expected to follow the rabbi so closely that they would be

covered with their master's whole way of thinking, living and acting.[6]

Thousands of years later, we're called to do the same. Though we walk on paved roads, not dusty ones, we are still called to be disciples — to follow our Rabbi, Jesus Christ, so closely that we are covered by the "dust" of his life, that we are changed and made new. These are exactly the kind of disciples that Jesus is looking for. He calls us to imitate him.

But how can we do that today?

The early disciples sought to imitate the life Jesus taught them in four ways: "[T]hey devoted themselves to the apostles' teaching and fellowship, to the breaking of the bread and the prayers" (Acts 2:42). We can think of these four key practices of a disciple — prayer, fellowship, the breaking of the bread (i.e., the sacraments) and the teaching of the apostles — as the places where we encounter Jesus' guidance and power today, just like in the early Church. They will help us to grow spiritually far beyond what we could ever do on our own.

These four practices of prayer, fellowship, the sacraments, and the apostles' teaching are like the fuel we can add to keep the fire of our faith growing. The more we live out these four things, the more we will encounter Jesus ever anew and coat ourselves in the dust of our Rabbi. For example:

[W]e ponder an aspect of the apostolic faith that stirs us to praise or challenges us to make a sacrifice. This helps us become more like Christ. We sense in prayer God calling us to change, be better in a certain area or trust him more. We experience his love and mercy in the sacraments and long to come back again. We encounter Jesus in fellowship with our neighbor, the poor, the suffering and other Christians who encourage us in the faith and provide many opportunities to grow in the love of Christ by loving the Christ who abides in them.[7]

———————————— **DISCUSS** ————————————

Looking at these four practices (prayer, fellowship, the sacraments, and the apostles' teaching), what steps do you need to take to be better "covered in the dust" of your Rabbi, Jesus Christ?

TAKE ACTION

Now that you've learned what it means to be a disciple of Jesus, you can begin taking some concrete steps toward becoming a more faithful disciple. Focus especially on how you can draw closer to Christ by making the four practices of Acts 2:42 a greater part of your life. The next several articles in this book can be helpful guides for learning how to incorporate these four practices in your daily life.

KEY CONCEPTS

Imitation: One key word that sums up the life of a disciple is "imitation." A disciple should be "covered in the dust of the Rabbi," constantly striving to imitate Christ.

In Acts 2:42, the four practices of a disciple of Jesus are

1. Prayer
2. Fellowship
3. The breaking of the bread
4. The teaching of the apostles.

ADDITIONAL RESOURCES

Into His Likeness: Be Transformed as a Disciple of Christ by Dr. Edward Sri

The Activated Disciple by Jeff Cavins

Catechism of the Catholic Church 1805–1845 : "The Human Virtues"

Notes:

[1] The following sections of this article are based on insights from Edward Sri, *Into His Likeness: Be Transformed as a Disciple* (San Francisco: Ignatius Press, 2017).

[2] Edward Sri, *Into His Likeness: Be Transformed as a Disciple* (San Francisco: Ignatius Press, 2017), 25.

[3] Ibid., 29.

[4] John Paul II, *Catechesi Tradendae*, accessed September 25, 2020, Vatican.va, 20.

[5] Edward Sri, *Into His Likeness: Be Transformed as a Disciple*, 5.

[6] Ibid., 30.

[7] Edward Sri, "In the Dust of the Rabbi: Clarifying Discipleship for Faith Formation Today," *Review. catechetics.com*, accessed November 18, 2020, https://review.catechetics.com/dust-rabbi-clarifying-discipleship-faith-formation-today.

Notes

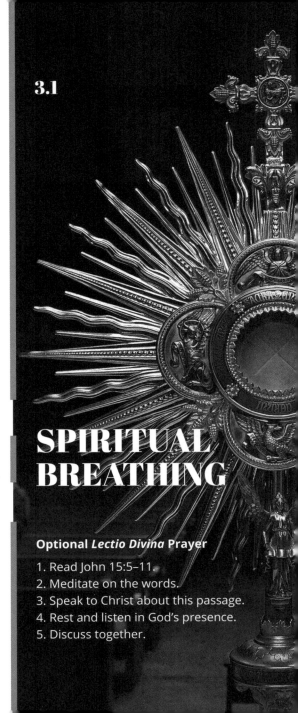

PRAYER

SPIRITUAL BREATHING

Optional *Lectio Divina* Prayer

1. Read John 15:5–11.
2. Meditate on the words.
3. Speak to Christ about this passage.
4. Rest and listen in God's presence.
5. Discuss together.

"If you are too busy to pray, you are too busy!"[1]

This was St. Mother Teresa's response to people who told her about the overwhelming amount of work in their lives. There were likely many moments when her sisters, the Missionaries of Charity, felt overwhelmed as they poured out their lives to care for the poorest of the poor around the world. But in 1973, Mother Teresa made a radical decision about how the sisters would use the little time they had each day in a new and extraordinary way.

The sisters were already very committed to prayer. As part of their regular routine, they stopped for prayer many times throughout the day: Morning Prayer, Mass, Midday Prayer, Evening Prayer and various devotions. But in 1973, Mother Teresa introduced into their daily schedule a "Holy Hour" — one hour of prayer in Eucharistic adoration, modeled after Jesus praying in the Garden of Gethsemane.

If our life is without prayer, it is like a house without a foundation.

— *St. Mother Teresa*

From a practical perspective, such a move seems counterintuitive. These sisters are doing some of the hardest work in the world, caring for the poorest of the poor around the globe. With so much need, so much work to be accomplished, why spend an extra hour in prayer each day?

To that concern, Mother Teresa replied, "If we don't take time to pray, we could not do this work."[2] She also described the effects of that time of prayer on her community: "This hour of intimacy with Jesus is something very beautiful. I have seen a great change in our congregation from the day we started having adoration every day. Our love for Jesus is more intimate. Our love for each other is more understanding. Our love for the poor is more compassionate."[3]

St. Mother Teresa clearly had a supernatural outlook on her life. She knew that her work depended not primarily on her own talent, ability, planning, and effort, but on allowing God to work through her. She knew how much she needed God, and that's one reason

why she committed herself to prayer each day. She was convinced that, on her own, she could accomplish very little, for Jesus himself says, "apart from me you can do nothing" (Jn 15:5).

DISCUSS

What stands out to you about St. Mother Teresa's commitment to prayer? Have you ever tried to make prayer a daily part of your busy schedule? How did it go?

SPIRITUAL BREATHING

We need time to pray each day if we want to grow spiritually. The soul needs prayer like the body needs oxygen. To be filled more with Christ's life, we need to take in what Pope Francis has called "the deep breath of prayer."[4]

But what exactly is prayer? The great saint of prayer, St. Teresa of Avila, said, "Mental prayer is nothing else, in my opinion, but being on terms of friendship with God, frequently conversing in secret with him who we know loves us."[5] Prayer is not a complicated formula or a series of rigid steps; it is our very relationship with God! According to the *Catechism*, "prayer is the living relationship of the children of God with their Father" (CCC 2565).

When we make daily prayer a priority, our lives are better. We are reminded of our identity as children of a good Father in heaven, and all that we do — our work, relationships, responsibilities — is enriched with Christ's Spirit. Rather than relying on our own abilities, efforts, and plans, it will be Christ radiating through us, filling us with the grace to live life in ways that are much more fulfilling than we could gain on our own.

Most of all, prayer is not about what we do so much as it is something God initiates as he puts a desire for him on our hearts. He put that desire for prayer in us because he longs for our time, our attention, and our love. "Jesus thirsts; his asking arises from the depths of God's desire for us. Whether we realize it or not, prayer is the encounter of God's thirst with ours. God thirsts that we may thirst for him" (CCC 2560).

Taking the leap to start a daily prayer life can be intimidating. But these three principles can help you get started.

Consistent

First, we must be *consistent*. Most great things in life all come about through a routine and consistent effort. Think of athletes training for competition. They practice the same actions repeatedly, every day, to master the habits of their sport. They have a consistent training regimen that allows them to succeed. Without consistency, they struggle to be successful.

We need to have something similar in mind for our life of prayer. When you are getting started, don't worry too much about all the details of prayer. To begin, simply make sure you have a consistent prayer time and routine each day. Even if you can pray for only ten minutes, find a way to do it every day so that you build up the habit, and through the habit build your relationship with God.

As you seek to build a habit of prayer, your consistency will be tested by busy schedules, competing priorities, or even feelings of boredom or frustration. In these times, you will need perseverance to continue in the daily life of relationship with God.

Quiet

Second, we need *quiet* in our hearts. When we talk to friends, we want to have their full attention. The same is true in the great conversation of prayer. God wants our full attention. He wants to hear what is on our heart — what we're going through, our hopes, our dreams, our fears, our hurts, our needs. He also wants to speak to us through his words in Scripture or the saints or other devotional books we might use in prayer. He wants to encourage us, comfort us, and prompt us.

But if we don't have enough silence in our souls, we won't be able to speak to him and we won't be able to listen to what he has to say to us. Find a quiet place — for example, in your room, in a chapel, outdoors — where you're less likely to be distracted. Put down your phone or even turn it off so you don't have the distractions of incessant notifications.

Apart from me you can do nothing.

— John 15:5

Simple

Third, we need a plan for prayer that's *simple*.

Many people ask, what am I supposed to do in prayer? While there are many different approaches and techniques to prayer, when you're first starting out, you want to keep it simple. After you quiet yourself down and recognize God's presence, take some time to read: perhaps a few verses from the Bible, a few lines from a saint, passages from a devotional book like *In Conversation with God* or *The Imitation of Christ* or meditations found in publications like *Magnificat*. Then, have a simple conversation with God about what is going on in the passage and how it relates to your life. Tell the Lord something that struck you about what you read. Ask him a question about it. Reflect on how it might apply to your life right now. Talk to God about it and take time in quiet to listen as well. Finally, take what you've learned in prayer and make a resolution for how you want to live better.

───────────────── **DISCUSS** ─────────────────

How have you prayed in the past? What was helpful as you tried to have a conversation with God?

LECTIO DIVINA

One simple and powerful way you can begin to pray is with a method known as *Lectio Divina*, which means "divine reading." It is a traditional Christian way of praying with sacred Scripture. Pope Benedict XVI once said, "If [*lectio divina*] is effectively promoted, this practice will bring to the Church — I am convinced of it — a new spiritual springtime."[6]

Lectio Divina consists of four stages:

1. *Lectio* **(Reading)**. As you begin, choose a short passage and read the passage slowly and prayerfully. Pay attention to a word or phrase that sticks out to you or catches your attention.

2. *Meditatio* **(Meditation)**. Read the passage again and, this time, pause to reflect on that part that stuck out to you. Prayerfully consider the meaning of the word or phrase and why this might have grabbed your attention.

3. *Oratio* **(Prayer)**. Read the passage a third time, and then turn to the Lord and speak to him about the passage. Ask him what he wants you to learn and how he might be inviting you change or draw closer to him.

4. *Contemplatio* **(Contemplation)**. In this final stage, rest in God's presence and in whatever graces, insights, encouragements, or challenges you received from God during this time of prayer. Thank him for the ways he spoke to you and resolve to remain close to him.

This model of prayer, when practiced regularly, will help you learn to hear God's voice, encounter him more deeply in the Scriptures and conform your life more to Christ. As the *Catechism* explains, "Seek in reading and you will find in meditating; knock in mental prayer and it will be opened to you by contemplation" (CCC 2654).

TAKE ACTION

Take a moment to practice praying *Lectio Divina* according to the steps above. Consider using the optional passage given at the beginning of this article.

Next, set a goal and plan how to incorporate some time of daily prayer into your life. Start simple and choose something attainable that you can do each day. One great way to build the habit of prayer is to pray at the same time and place as someone who already prays each day. It will add instant accountability for sticking to your commitment. For the first few times, this person might even share how they pray so that you can continue to learn.

At the end of this article, you will find FOCUS' Prayer Challenge. The goal is simple: to pray every day for 30 days with a passage from Scripture. Typically, habits can be formed by doing something consistently for one month; by completing the Prayer Challenge, you will have a much better chance of making prayer, and a deeper friendship with God, a foundational part of your life. If you would like to embrace this challenge, make a plan and get started, possibly with a friend for added accountability!

KEY CONCEPTS

Spiritual Breathing: We must take in "the deep breath of prayer" each day. The soul needs prayer like the body needs oxygen.

Relationship: Prayer is relationship with God (CCC 2558).

3 Principles for Daily Prayer: Consistent, Quiet, Simple

ADDITIONAL RESOURCES

Time for God by Fr. Jacques Philippe

WRAP Yourself in Scripture by Karen L. Dwyer

Meditation and Contemplation by Timothy M. Gallagher, O.M.V.

Pocket Guide to Adoration by Fr. Josh Johnson

CCC 2560–2865: "Christian Prayer"

Notes

[1] Jim Towey, "It All Begins with Prayer," *Columbia* (July 2010): 13, https://www.kofc.org/un/en/resources/mother-teresa/columbia-excerpts072010.pdf.

[2] Joyce Coronel, "Too Busy to Pray? Finding Time for God Brings Peace," *Catholicsun.org* (May 14, 2012): https://www. catholicsun.org/2012/05/14/too-busy-to-pray-finding-time-for-god-brings-peace/.

[3] Mother Teresa, *No Greater Love* (California: New World Library, 1995), 154.

[4] Francis, *Evangelii Gaudium,* accessed February 25, 2020, Vatican.va, 262.

[5] St. Teresa of Avila, *The Way of Perfection*, trans. Kieran Kavanaugh, O.C.D. and Otilio Rodriguez, O.C.D. (Washington, D.C.: ICS Publications, 2000).

[6] Benedict XVI, "Address of His Holiness Benedict XVI to the Participants in the International Congress Organized to Commemorate the 40th Anniversary of the Dogmatic Constitution on Divine Revelation 'Dei Verbum,'" accessed February 25, 2020, Vatican.va.

SUPPLEMENTAL RESOURCE

3.1 PRAYER: SPIRITUAL BREATHING

30-DAY PRAYER CHALLENGE

Part 1: Jesus' Early Life

Luke 1:26–35
Luke 1:36–45
Luke 1:46–56
Luke 2:1–20
Luke 3:15–23
Luke 4:1–15
Luke 5:1–11

Part 2: Jesus' Ministry

Luke 6:12–26
Luke 6:27–38
Luke 6:43–49
Luke 7:36–50
Luke 8:4–15
Luke 8:22–25
Luke 9:18–27

Part 3: Jesus on the Road to Jerusalem

Luke 9:51–62
Luke 10:38–42
Luke 11:1–13
Luke 11:37–44
Luke 12:22–31
Luke 15:1–2; 11–26
Luke 18:1–8

Part 4: Jesus' Death

Luke 22:14–23
Luke 22:39–46
Luke 22:54–62
Luke 23:13–25
Luke 23:32–43
Luke 23:44–56

Part 5: Jesus' Resurrection

Luke 24:1–12
Luke 24:13–35
Luke 24:36–53

Notes

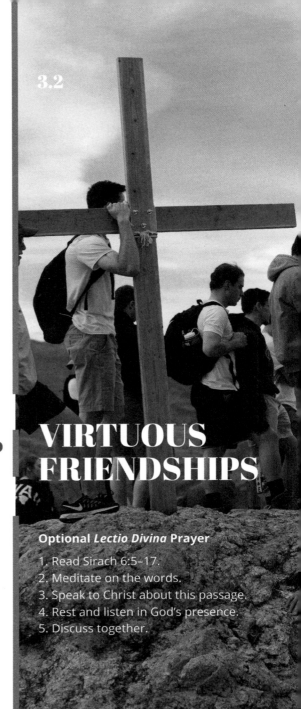

3.2

FELLOWSHIP

VIRTUOUS FRIENDSHIPS

Optional *Lectio Divina* Prayer

1. Read Sirach 6:5–17.
2. Meditate on the words.
3. Speak to Christ about this passage.
4. Rest and listen in God's presence.
5. Discuss together.

On a cold night in the fourth century A.D., forty young Roman soldiers huddled together while immersed in a freezing lake.

Notes

Licinius, the pagan emperor, was persecuting them for their Christian faith. As a result, they now faced death and the biggest temptation of their lives: They could go free at any moment if they chose to worship the pagan gods. As an added enticement, the lake was directly across from the Roman baths. As the soldiers' bodies shook and their teeth chattered, they could see the steam from the hot pools rising into the freezing air. In the midst of this torture, the soldiers had one unified prayer: "Lord, we are forty engaged in this contest. Grant that forty may receive crowns and that we may not fall short of that sacred number."[1]

Throughout the night, this band of brothers was tempted to give in. Unable to resist any longer, one soldier headed for the baths only to die instantly upon arrival. One of the guards who was keeping watch was so moved by their witness that he removed his clothes and joined them in the icy lake. All forty of these remained faithful unto death, an answer to the men's prayer.

The story of these soldiers served as an inspiration to the power of Christian fellowship throughout the Roman Empire, and they were immortalized by the Catholic Church as the Martyrs of San Sebaste.

DISCUSS

What stands out to you in this story? What do you think allowed these men to remain faithful?

HOT COALS

The friendships of these men allowed them to remain heroically faithful to Christ. You most likely won't find yourself in the same

A faithful friend is a sturdy shelter: he that has found one has found a treasure.

— Sirach 6:14

situation as these Roman soldiers, but you need Christian friendship just as much as they did. If you don't have close friends who are Christians, there's a good chance you won't grow in your relationship with Christ.

Think about a charcoal fire. When the coals are piled together, each coal remains hotter for a longer period. The coals help each other remain on fire. Conversely, when a coal becomes separated from the others, it cools more quickly. Like hot coals, we need other Christians around us to remain "on fire" for Christ.

The Martyrs of San Sebaste in that freezing lake were like a group of hot coals. There had to be countless times when the men wanted to go to shore, overwhelmed by the frigid conditions. They surely thought of their families, their wives, and their children. But because they were together, these men were able to encourage and support one another. When they were tempted to renounce Christ, someone was there to remind them of the heavenly crown that awaited them. As a group, these men were able to remain faithful, something that might have been impossible if they didn't have support from one another.

DISCUSS

Do you have "hot coals" in your life? Are you a "hot coal" for others?

THREE KINDS OF FRIENDSHIPS

Since the very beginning of the Church, the early Christians considered fellowship to be one of four foundational practices of the Christian life (Acts 2:42). We need this same habit in our own lives. But how do we experience this kind of friendship? The first step is to know what kind of friends we are looking for and what kind of friends we need to be.

Many people in our lives claim to have some type of friendship with us, but do we have friends who are committed to us and to what's truly best for us? Do we have friends who will push us in the right direction?

The ancient Greek philosopher Aristotle taught that there are three kinds of friendships.[2]

- **Friendship of Utility**

   The first type is a *friendship of utility*, one based on some benefit or advantage found in the relationship. Business relationships, group projects in class, and other transactional exchanges often fall under this category. Think about your favorite coffee shop: You go there because you enjoy the coffee, and the coffee shop serves you because they make money. You might get to know the people working there. They might sincerely take an interest in your life and engage in friendly conversation with you. These basic levels of friendship are common in life. But the relationship is primarily built on the benefit the coffee shop receives from you (business) and the benefit you receive from the coffee shop (good coffee).

- **Friendship of Pleasure**

   The second type of friendship is *friendship of pleasure*, one based primarily on the fun times two people share together. For example, two people might happen to live near each other, play on the same team, visit the same restaurant, or belong to the same parish. They might like the same music, the same sports team, the same television show, or the same party scenes. These kinds of friendships are based primarily on the fun they have spending time with each other.

While these first two types of friendships are not bad in themselves, Aristotle notes how they are the most fragile and least likely to last the test of time, because these friends are not committed to the other as a person, seeking what's best for them. These friends are more committed to the benefit, pleasure, or fun time they get from the relationship. For example, when your classes or interests change, you shift roles or locations at work or you are no longer involved in the same activities or frequenting that particular coffee shop, your friendship is not likely to continue. The benefit or fun times are no longer there, so unless there's something deeper uniting you, you are unlikely to share a deeply committed friendship.

While these basic forms of friendships are common in life, especially when we are young, it's important to know that they often dissolve when life grows difficult and the friendship no longer brings the enjoyment, fun times, benefit, or convenience that the other person is looking for. You can probably think of examples of these kinds of friendships in your own life and how quickly some of them have come and gone.

● *Virtuous Friendship*

According to Aristotle, the third kind of friendship is friendship in the fullest sense. He calls it *virtuous friendship*. This is based on something much deeper: The friend is committed to *you* and *your* good, not just to some benefit or enjoyment that they receive from being with you. The virtuous friend loves you in the true sense of the word: *They seek what is best for you*, which is to live a virtuous life in imitation of Christ and eventually live forever with him in heaven. As Christians, this is the highest form of fellowship and should be our aim in our own friendships.

For a virtuous friendship to develop, both people must be striving for virtue. They don't need to be perfect, but they do need to be pursuing the virtuous life together. They also need to be involved in each other's lives. Simply clicking "friend" on social media or interacting through screens is not how virtuous friendships form. In Christian friendships, when both people are striving to deepen their relationship with God and live like Christ, they help each other in what matters most in life. A true friend wants you to live out your faith to the fullest. Because of this, it is essential for you to find brothers and sisters in Christ who can help ensure that your faith not only survives but thrives.

DISCUSS

Which friendships in your life are virtuous friendships? Which ones are merely friendships of utility or pleasure?

"AS IRON SHARPENS IRON"

We can, of course, have different levels of friendship with people in different areas of life, regardless of whether they are Christian. While not every single friendship we have needs to be the deepest friendship, we want to make sure we do have close Christian friends who are running after the same goals, friends who can help strengthen us in our faith. After all, we become like the people we associate with most. And that challenges us to ask an important question: Are our closest friends going to help us become the kind of people we want to become?

Proverbs 27:17 says, "Iron sharpens iron, and one man sharpens another." When a sword gets dull, it cannot be sharpened easily; it takes another iron tool to sharpen it back into precision. In our own lives, we need strong, virtuous friends who can help us smooth the rough edges of our faults and sharpen us in virtue. And a sword is an excellent analogy for the battle each one of us must face in

keeping the faith: If we allow our faith to grow dull and weak, we are going to snap under the pressure of this world. However, if we have fellowship, we will be sharp enough not only to resist temptation but to grow even stronger.

Over and over, we see this dynamic played out in the lives of the saints. It's been said that saints come in clusters: Whenever you read about a saint, you discover that they rarely became a saint on their own. Usually, other saints were right by their side, sharpening them in the process. Their intense fellowship spurred them to pursue a deeper holiness and increased their desire to share Jesus with others, even in difficult circumstances. St. Francis Xavier had St. Ignatius of Loyola; St. Teresa of Avila had St. John of the Cross; St. Felicity had St. Perpetua. Whom do you have? Finding virtuous friends can help you get to heaven and make a deeper impact for Christ here on earth.

Sometimes, we are also called to make changes in our friendships. If the people we are spending time with aren't leading us closer to Christ — if they aren't "sharpening" us — we might have to make some tough decisions. While we shouldn't abandon these friends, we can't allow them to lead us away from the Faith, either. This might require us to change the amount of time we spend with these friends or change the activities we do with them. Also, we may not be able to rely on these friends in the most important areas of our lives because they aren't yet thinking with the mind of Christ. This process of change can be difficult, but as Christians, we need friends who will make us sharper, not duller.

We can certainly invite our non-Catholic friends to experience the love of Christ themselves. We have a unique opportunity to call these friends to conversion. How much better it is when these friends get to hear the Gospel from someone they know and trust! And how beautiful it is when our non-Christian friends come to know Jesus and become friends who can also help us draw closer to him!

Notes

DISCUSS

Are you and your friends helping each other become saints? How so? Do you need to make any changes in your friendships?

TAKE ACTION

Make a plan for better fellowship. Now that you've read about what constitutes virtuous friendship and Christian fellowship, take steps to develop these relationships in your life. Take some time to reflect on these two questions, and make a plan for improving your friendships:

- *Which relationships need to grow?* Who is helping me become a saint, and how can I spend more time with this person/these people?

- *Which relationships might need to change?* How are other friendships in my life holding me back from a life of virtue? What changes should I make? How can I invite these friends to virtuous friendship instead of merely friendships of utility or pleasure?

KEY CONCEPTS

Hot Coals Analogy: Like hot coals, we need other Christians for us to remain "on fire" for Christ.

Aristotle's Three Kinds of Friendship:

- *Friendship of Utility*: Friendship based on some benefit the person gets from you

- *Friendship of Pleasure*: Friendship based on enjoyment or "fun times" someone shares with you

- *Virtuous Friendship*: Friendship based not on what someone gets from you, but on a commitment to you as a person and seeking what is best for you, which is the virtuous life

Iron Sharpens Iron: "Iron sharpens iron, and one man sharpens another" (Prv 27:17).

ADDITIONAL RESOURCES

True Friendship: Where Virtue Becomes Happiness by John Cuddeback

The Four Loves by C.S. Lewis

Notes

[1] Bert Ghezzi, *Voices of the Saints* (Chicago: Loyola Press, 2009), 225.

[2] Aristotle, *Nichomachean Ethics*, trans. W.D. Ross, VIII.3, last modified 2009, http://classics.mit.edu/Aristotle/nicomachaen.html.

Notes

SACRAMENTS

THE EUCHARIST

Optional *Lectio Divina* Prayer

1. Read Luke 22:14–23.
2. Meditate on the words.
3. Speak to Christ about this passage.
4. Rest and listen in God's presence.
5. Discuss together.

Notes

T he Chinese authorities burst into the church. The commander ordered the soldiers to tear down the tabernacle from the sanctuary.[1]

They opened the tabernacle and scattered the consecrated hosts across the floor. The men trampled on the Eucharist, while the commander sneered at the crowd: "Do you still believe in those fairytales your priest told you?"[2]

The soldiers arrested the priest and locked him in a metal bunker inside the church. Trapped, he peered out through a small slit, watching as he saw his people forced outside. He could see the Eucharistic hosts left desecrated on the church floor.

For days, the church remained totally silent. Guards were posted around the church, and no one was allowed to enter. But one day, the priest looked through the slit in the bunker where he was confined and saw someone sneaking into the church. It was a young girl, 13 years old, kneeling in prayer, crawling on her hands and knees toward the hosts on the floor. She bent down and received a single host on the tongue, prayed for a while, and then left.

The next day, the little girl returned, taking one more host. She did this daily, receiving one host at a time. For a month, she entered the church each day, risking being caught by the authorities. Finally, only one host remained. She entered the church again to receive it. She made her prayers as usual, but shortly after she leaned down and received Jesus for the last time, she made a slight noise. The guard heard her, and the church doors burst open behind her. The priest heard a shot and saw the body of the young girl fall to the floor.

She died as a martyr, giving her life for Jesus in the Holy Eucharist. As he pondered the little girl's witness, that same soldier was struck to the heart; inspired by her faith, he later came and let the priest free from the bunker. The soldier told the priest, "If in every city there were one such girl as this one, there would not be a soldier left who would fight for Communism."[3]

——————————— **DISCUSS** ———————————

Does this story change your perception of what it means to be devoted to Jesus in the Eucharist? How so?

REAL PRESENCE

What this little girl did makes no sense at all if the Eucharist is just a piece of bread. But she saw something more in those consecrated hosts. This was not bread. She understood the real presence of Jesus in the Eucharist — the fact that the bread and wine at Mass are changed into Christ's Body and Blood. And it was this truth that drove her to risk her life to protect Jesus in the Eucharist from further desecration.

The Eucharist is the source and summit of the Christian life.

—CCC 1324

But where do Catholics get this idea of the real presence? If you had to explain the Catholic belief in the Eucharist to someone else, could you do it? Could you explain how something that looks, feels, and tastes like bread and wine is really Jesus' Body and Blood? And where in the Bible does Jesus ever teach about such a mysterious doctrine as this? Whether you've heard this teaching long ago or this is a new concept to you, this mystery of the Eucharist is so central that we can never ponder its awesome reality enough — lest we become the kind of people who take for granted the greatest gift Jesus left us before he died.

First, let's make sure we clearly understand the doctrine itself. Since the time of the apostles, Christians have believed that the bread and wine at Mass are changed into Christ's Body and Blood. But this is not a chemical change. If you put the consecrated host under a microscope, you would see all the chemical properties of bread. But Catholics for 2,000 years have believed what that young girl in China believed and died for: that, during the Last Supper on the night before he died, Jesus took bread and said "This is my body..." — and underneath those outward, sensible appearances of bread is the very Body, Blood, Soul, and Divinity of Christ.

Second, we need to grasp clearly the biblical foundations for the Eucharist. While many Scriptural passages shed light on this mystery, there's one in particular that gives the richest insights. Let's look at chapter 6 of John's Gospel, where Jesus delivers his clearest teaching about the Eucharist.

Although many non-Catholic Christians think of the Eucharist in a purely symbolic way — that the Eucharist is just a symbol of Jesus' Body and Blood or a sacred reminder of Christ — Jesus tells the crowds something different in this scene from John. He says that he is the true Bread of Life and that they must eat his flesh and drink his blood if they want to have eternal life. That's strong language. And it's clear he's not speaking merely in a figurative or metaphorical way: He's speaking literally. He really wants us to partake of his Body and Blood.

Consider Jesus' own words: "I am the living bread which came down from heaven ... and the bread which I shall give for the life of the world *is my flesh*" (Jn 6:51; emphasis added). Here, it is clear that the crowds understand Jesus' words literally. They're appalled, saying, "How can this man give us his flesh to eat?" (Jn 6:52). Notice how Jesus doesn't try to clear up a misunderstanding, soften his language, or say he was just speaking metaphorically. He instead presses the issue further: "Truly, truly, I say to you, unless you eat the flesh of the Son of Man and drink his blood, you have no life in you" (Jn 6:53).

Next, Jesus goes on to use a more graphic word for "eat," meaning "to gnaw" or "to chew" in verses 54–57. He says, "He who *eats* [chews] my flesh and drinks my blood will have eternal life" (Jn 6:54). He wouldn't talk this way if he was only speaking metaphorically about the Eucharist — as if the Eucharist was supposed to be just a symbol of his presence. If anything, he's making his statement more literal. Indeed, he goes on to state explicitly, "For my flesh is food indeed, and my blood is drink indeed. He who eats my flesh and drinks my blood abides in me, and I in him" (Jn 6:55–56). Jesus is clear: This is his flesh and blood.

We can see from the crowd's response that they clearly understood Jesus in this literal way. They grumbled and complained about this radical idea. Even "many of his disciples drew back and no longer went about with him" (Jn 6:66). If the Eucharist were just a symbol, why didn't Jesus call them all back, saying, "Wait, I was only speaking figuratively!"? Instead, he lets them go. He loves us so much that he is not willing to compromise on his supreme gift to us — the gift of his very Body and Blood in the Eucharist.

--------- **DISCUSS** ---------

Do you believe in the real presence? Could you explain it to someone else? What difference does this truth make in your life?

LOVE NEAR US

Love wants to be near the one it loves. And the God who is love ardently longs to be close to us. That's why he dwells among us here on Earth in the Eucharist.

The presence of that divine love in Christ had a powerful impact on people's lives 2,000 years ago in Galilee. It overcame illness, drove away darkness, brought healing to those who were suffering, shared forgiveness in the face of sin. Did you know we can encounter that same powerful presence of Jesus in the Eucharist? And we can encounter him not only when we receive him in Holy Communion at Mass, but also when we draw near to him in all the tabernacles in all our Catholic churches around the world.

If you want to draw near to divine love himself and experience the power of his real presence in your life — the power to guide, comfort, and strengthen you — receive Jesus in the Eucharist as often as you can and visit him in the chapel where he continues to reside in the tabernacle, where the sacred hosts are kept.

Do we approach Holy Communion with the same reverence and devotion that the little Chinese girl had? She went to such great lengths, even risking her own life, to draw near to Christ's presence in the Eucharist, to love him in Eucharistic adoration, and receive him in Communion each day. Do you have that same desire? What sacrifices are you willing to make to draw near to him?

Jesus in the Eucharist is readily available to you in your own parish. Have you ever thought of going to Mass not just on Sunday, but also during the week to receive him? Do you make the effort in your busy day to stop by the chapel, to tell him you love him, to bring your needs to him, to rest in his presence? Jesus is waiting for you in this sacrament. He longs for you to come to him.

> *The greatest love story of all time is contained in a tiny white host.*
>
> — *Venerable Archbishop Fulton Sheen*

DISCUSS

Jesus desires to draw close to you. Do you have that same desire to draw close to him? What sacrifices do you need to make to be more devoted to Jesus in the Eucharist?

TAKE ACTION

Take some time to research parish locations and Mass times near you. Are you committed to attending Sunday Mass each week? If you do not attend regularly, decide on a parish and make a plan to go. Think about any obstacles that might prevent you. How can you ensure that those things don't get in your way to attend Sunday Mass?

Can you begin to make going to daily Mass a part of your life as well? It might not be the most convenient, but the things that are best for us rarely are. Consider how your schedule could change for you to attend daily Mass more frequently.

Finally, a beautiful way we can grow in our devotion to the Eucharist is by visiting Jesus in the tabernacles of our churches or in Eucharistic adoration. Which churches near you offer times of adoration? Brainstorm a time in your day or your week that you could do your prayer time in front of the Blessed Sacrament.

KEY CONCEPTS

Real Presence: The Eucharist is truly the Body and Blood of Jesus.

Frequent Communion/Visits to the Blessed Sacrament: Jesus longs for us to encounter him regularly in the Eucharist.

ADDITIONAL RESOURCES

Jesus and the Jewish Roots of the Eucharist by Dr. Brant Pitre

A Biblical Walk through the Mass by Dr. Edward Sri

CCC 1322–1419: "The Sacrament of the Eucharist"

SEEK2015 Talk on focusequip.org: "The Hour That Will Change Your Life" by Fr. Mike Schmitz

Jesus, Present Before Me: Meditations for Eucharistic Adoration by Fr. Peter John Cameron, O.P.

Notes

[1] This story is adapted from: Karl Maria Harrer, *Die schönsten Eucharistischen Wunder* (Miriam-Verlog, 1990, vol. 1 – 5).

[2] "The Little Girl Who Inspired Archbishop Fulton Sheen's Vow," *America Needs Fatima*, accessed February 25, 2020, https://www.americaneedsfatima.org/Conversions/the-little-girl-who-inspired-archbishop-fulton-sheen-s-vow.html.

[3] Ibid.

SACRAMENTS

THE HEALING POWER OF CONFESSION

Optional *Lectio Divina* Prayer

1. Read John John 8:3–11.
2. Meditate on the words.
3. Speak to Christ about this passage.
4. Rest and listen in God's presence.
5. Discuss together.

I n fourth-century Milan, there lived a talented professor of rhetoric.

While one of his parents continually tried to get him to convert to Christianity, he had decided to follow some of the pagan philosophies of his day. Thankfully, through a series of friendships, the professor began to reconsider Christianity, and over time, he became convinced that it was true.

There was just one problem: His attachment to sexual sin overwhelmed him and kept him from conversion.

The professor tried to forget about his struggle until, one day, a simple Christian man named Ponticianus came to his house for business. Upon seeing the professor's copy of St. Paul's epistles, Ponticianus told the story of how he had converted to the Catholic Faith. While they were speaking, the professor was reminded of his own struggles and became ashamed that he, who was much smarter, more successful, and more famous, was unable to do what his simple friend had nobly done: give up his sins and start living as a Christian.

After saying goodbye to Ponticianus, the professor went into his garden to weep. There he considered the choice that lay before him: He could remain on the fence with his faith, believing in his head but not following God in his heart in how he lived each day — or he could turn his life around and commit to following Christ.

His mind began to race. On the one hand, his lust taunted him: He realized that, if he chose Christ, he would have to give up sexual sin forever. On the other hand, the life of chastity also began to appeal to him: He recalled the many Christian men and women who were able to rise above their slavery to lust because God gave them the strength to do what they could not do on their own.

During this interior battle, the professor heard voices of children playing and repeating the phrase, "take and read, take and read."

The children's words inspired him to pick up his book of St. Paul's epistles and read the first passage he found. He read: "[L]et us conduct ourselves becomingly as in the day, not in reveling and drunkenness, not in debauchery and licentiousness, not in quarreling and jealousy. But put on the Lord Jesus Christ, and make no provision for the flesh, to gratify its desires" (Rom 13:13–14).

A light of certainty flooded the professor's heart, and all his doubt faded away. He repented of his sins, was baptized, and eventually became a priest and then a bishop. He became one of the greatest saints and theologians that the Church has ever known: St. Augustine of Hippo. His autobiography — *Confessions*, where he tells his story — is one of the most read books in history.

———————————————— **DISCUSS** ————————————————

What is your initial reaction to the story of St. Augustine? Do you notice people having similar struggles today?

REPENTANCE

Repentance is a key disposition in the Christian life. In Scripture, the word "repent" (*metanoia*) means to "turn around" or "turn back." It involves a fundamental turning around in our life, turning away from sin and turning toward Christ. The Catholic Church explains it this way: "Interior repentance is a radical reorientation of our whole life, a return, a conversion to God with all our heart, an end to sin, a turning away from evil, with repugnance toward the evil actions we have committed" (CCC 1431).

Repentance is necessary to remain in right relationship with God, our loving Father and creator. The sin in our hearts should cause us great sorrow because sin separates us from God. Our sin motivates us to repent so that we can return to union with him.

But repentance is not a one-time act. It's an ongoing habit for a disciple of Jesus who wants to grow. The Bible challenges us, "rend your hearts" (Jl 2:13), which means to tear open our hearts, to look inside and see what's really there. Then we must have the courage to remove anything that does not belong in the heart of a Christian. Whether it's big sins like the sexual impurity Augustine struggled with or the hundreds of petty sins that plague many Christians — little grudges we hold, a tendency to complain, envy, self-centeredness, lack of kindness, lack of trust, pride, discouragement, wasting time — we all have plenty of sins in our hearts of which we can repent!

But there are several things that can hold us back from true repentance. Let's look at three.

Rationalization: I Don't Need to Repent

First, we might not think we have much to repent of. Our relativistic culture often avoids talking about what is right or wrong. Because of this, it is easy to look at our own lives and think, "I'm a good person. I haven't committed any horrible crimes. Everyone else does this. I know other people who are much worse than I am." But God doesn't grade on a curve. True disciples of Jesus don't try to rationalize their sin. When a part of us senses we might have done something wrong or we're doing something that goes against what Jesus and his Church teaches, the next step is to repent: to admit our fault, trust in God's mercy, and try to change our behavior instead of trying to justify our sins, convincing ourselves what we're doing is okay.

Fear of Repenting: I Don't Want to Change!

Second, we might be afraid to let go of certain sins. Augustine knew what he was doing was wrong, but he didn't want to give up his bad habits. Before his conversion, he once even prayed, "Lord, give me chastity... only not yet!"[1] We, too, might be afraid to give up a sin, perhaps because we fear what others will think of us or we wonder whether life will lose its fun. But we need to see what Augustine came to see: that God's plan is for our happiness, and when we follow God's plan, we always find a greater joy than we would otherwise, no matter the cost. The joy of the Gospel is so much better than our sins.

Despair: I Can't Be Forgiven

Third, we might doubt we are capable of repentance. Like Augustine, we might believe we are so enslaved to sin that turning our lives around is impossible. We might delay and convince ourselves that, maybe later when we have our lives put together, we can repent and believe in God. Jesus, however, doesn't work like this. We don't need to "put our lives in order" so that we can begin living in friendship with Jesus; we need to entrust our lives to Jesus so that he can put our lives in order! We cannot do it on our own. But with his help, we can be forgiven, changed, and made new.

Sometimes we are so ashamed of our sins — sexual sins, addictions, bad habits, or other serious offenses — that we think it's impossible for God to forgive us. However, this is a lie. In fact, compared to the ocean of God's mercy, our sins are like a single drop of water. God's mercy totally envelops our sins, no matter how serious. He always forgives when we come seeking his mercy.

DISCUSS

If you were to rend your heart open and look inside, what weakness would you find there that separates you most often from God? Which of these three obstacles — rationalization, fear of letting go of certain sins or thinking you can't change — might hold you back from true repentance?

CONFESSION

A crucial step toward full repentance is going to confession. For many Catholics, confession is one of the most freeing, liberating, life-giving experiences of their lives. Instead of holding on to the burden of their sin and guilt, they are able to give it to God, who not only forgives them, but also embraces them as a loving Father and rejoices at their returning home, just like in Jesus' Parable of the Prodigal Son (Lk 15:11–32).

For some people, however, confession is scary and misunderstood. We might be hesitant to confess our sins, afraid of what the priest might think. Or we may not understand this sacrament, thinking, "Why confess to a priest? Isn't God the one who forgives me?" Or maybe we are just nervous and unsure of how to make a good confession. Let's address some of these concerns.

First, the sacrament of reconciliation (confession) is instituted by Christ as the place he wants us to go to deal with our sins. Jesus said to his apostles, "Receive the Holy Spirit. If you forgive the sins of any, they are forgiven; if you retain the sins of any, they are retained" (Jn 20:22–23). Just as the Father sent Jesus to forgive the sins of the world, so too are his apostles (and their successors) called to forgive sins.

But why did Jesus set it up this way, instead of simply having us pray to God? Why involve a priest?

God has always used human beings as instruments in his plan of salvation. Whether it was Moses leading the people out of Egypt or the prophet Elijah raising a girl from the dead, God has worked through his human leaders, even if they are fallen and sinful. Therefore, we shouldn't be surprised when we see God still involving his leaders, the priests and bishops, in his work today. Think of the priest in confession as God's instrument of mercy — or, in the words of St. Paul, "God's fellow worker" (1 Cor 3:9) — and having a "ministry of reconciliation" (2 Cor 5:19). It's not the priest who is forgiving our sins, but Jesus working through the priest.

A second reason confession is so important is that Scripture tells us to "confess [our] sins to one another" (Jas 5:16). When we have to verbalize our sins to another person, we are forced to face the truth about ourselves at a much deeper level. We speak our sins. We name them. And we do so in the presence of God's representative here on earth, the priest. We also have the privilege of hearing the priest say, "Your sins are forgiven. Go in peace." It's so important to hear those words, to have confidence that God has indeed forgiven us. Some of the most profound moments in friendship or marriage come when we say, "I am sorry," and we hear our friend or our beloved say, "I forgive you." How much more profound it is when we speak the words "I am sorry" not just in the silence of our hearts, but out loud to God's representative, the priest — and how much more beautiful it is when we hear Christ say to us through the priest, "I absolve you of all your sins"!

A third reason to go to confession regularly is that the sacrament gives us grace to heal and overcome our weaknesses. God doesn't just pardon our sins in confession: He gets to the root of our sins and heals our deeper wounds. This is another reason we should desire to go to confession regularly, at least once a month.

Finally, sometimes people are just nervous about going to confession or don't know what to do once they get there. There are plenty of guides to confession available; see the "Additional Resources" section for some options. As you prepare, don't be afraid to ask for help! Friends, leaders in your church or even the priest himself during your confession can help you make a great confession.

Jesus doesn't want you to remain stuck in your sin. He has a great plan for you. Don't let your sins hold you back. Come to him in confession and receive Christ's forgiveness, healing, and grace to overcome your weaknesses.

Notes

> *Be ashamed when you sin. Do not be ashamed when you repent.*
>
> — *St. John Chrysostom*

DISCUSS

How long has it been since you have been to confession? Do you have any hesitations about confession? Take some time to discuss how to make a good confession and any struggles you might have with receiving this sacrament.

TAKE ACTION

If you haven't been to confession in a while, consider how you could partake of this sacrament soon. When is confession offered at a parish close to you? How might you need to prepare? Feel free to reach out to a priest if you would feel more comfortable talking with someone before you go. You can also ask a friend to help you prepare and possibly go with you.

If you don't yet go to confession regularly, try to make a plan to go at least once a month. Look up confession times nearby and plan for when and where you will go to confession.

Finally, look up a good examination of conscience to help you prepare. See the "Additional Resources" section of this article for some suggestions.

KEY CONCEPTS

Repent: The word "repent" (*metanoia*) means to turn our whole lives around, to turn away from sin and toward Christ.

Apostolic Authority: Jesus gave his apostles the authority to forgive sins, and that was passed on to their successors throughout the centuries to the bishops and priests today: "Receive the Holy Spirit. If you forgive the sins of any, they are forgiven; if you retain the sins of any, they are retained" (Jn 20:22–23).

Frequent Confession: Not only are we forgiven of our sins, but we also receive grace to help us overcome our weaknesses and heal the wounds of sin in our lives.

ADDITIONAL RESOURCES

CCC 1422–1498: "The Sacrament of Penance and Reconciliation"

Lord Have Mercy: The Healing Power of Confession by Dr. Scott Hahn

From the FOCUS Blog on focusequip.org: "Confession Week (And Every Resource You'll Need)"

Notes

Notes

[1] Augustine of Hippo. *Confessions*, Book VIII, trans. Edward Bouverie Pusey, *Sacredtexts.com*, accessed April 2, 2020, https://www.sacred-texts.com/chr/augconf/aug08.htm.

THE APOSTLES' TEACHING

THE BATTLE FOR YOUR MIND

Optional *Lectio Divina* Prayer

1. Read Proverbs 2:1–5.
2. Meditate on the words.
3. Speak to Christ about this passage.
4. Rest and listen in God's presence.
5. Discuss together.

A conversation between Jesus and Pontius Pilate on Good Friday reveals two different ways of looking at reality.

Jesus of Nazareth says he comes to bear witness to the truth (Jn 18:37). Pilate sarcastically responds, "What is truth?" (Jn 18:38).

The idea of truth — a truth that applies to everyone, a truth that points to what is right and wrong and illuminates the path to human happiness — was not something Pilate cared about. Pilate knew Jesus was innocent and that the real reason the Jewish authorities were accusing him was because they were envious (Mt 27:18).

But the truth of Jesus' innocence didn't matter. Pilate had "his own truth": He wanted to save his career. The Jewish leaders were threatening him, saying, "If you release this man, you are not Caesar's friend" (Jn 19:12). Pilate feared a riot would break out, and he had to protect his reputation before Caesar's authority. So, to advance his own interests, he appeased the crowds and sent an innocent man away to be crucified.

Without truth as a compass, we make our choices based on fears, passions, emotions, and whims. We do whatever we want without asking the question of truth — without asking whether what we want is good or whether it will lead us to lasting happiness and to becoming the kind of person we want to be.

Pilate's "What is truth?" philosophy of life may be attractive to some in our modern world, but we must remember that truth is not an abstract idea. Truth is a Person, Jesus Christ: "In Jesus Christ, the whole of God's truth has been made manifest" (CCC 2466). After all, Jesus is not merely one of the world's many moral teachers; he is God become man. He doesn't simply show us a way *to* God; he *is* the way. And he doesn't just reveal truth *about* God; he *is* the truth. He came into the world to bear witness to the truth so that we might know how to be happy in this life and live with him forever in heaven: "For this I was born, and for this I have come into the world, to bear witness to the truth" (Jn 18:37).

So here's the crucial question every Christian must face: Will we truly follow Jesus as "the way, the truth and the life" (Jn 14:6) and allow his teachings to shape our lives — or will we follow in the footsteps of Pilate, who preferred to make up his own "truth"?

—————————————— **DISCUSS** ——————————————

Have you ever encountered Pilate's "What is truth?" philosophy? How does it show up in our modern culture today? What does it mean to say that Jesus is the truth, and what implications does this have for us as disciples?

DO NOT BE CONFORMED TO THIS WORLD

If Jesus is the truth, it changes the way we view the popular opinions and philosophies we encounter in our world. Like the early Christians who lived in a pagan world that always competed for their attention, we too face a constant battle for how we look at reality: what love is, what makes us happy, where we come from, where we're going, what life is all about.

Today's relativistic culture likes to portray itself as neutral, open-minded toward all viewpoints, promoting tolerance and acceptance. But the idea that "what's good for you is good for you, and what's good for me is good for me" is, in fact, *not* a neutral value. It is a specific way of looking at the world that rejects objective truth and opposes Jesus as the way, the truth, and the life — and it is being ceaselessly promoted in today's world.

Before becoming pope, Cardinal Ratzinger said,

> Today, having a clear faith based on the Creed of the Church is often labeled as fundamentalism. Whereas relativism, that is, letting oneself be "tossed here and there, carried about by every wind of doctrine," seems the only attitude that can cope with modern times. We are building a dictatorship of relativism that does not recognize anything as definitive and whose ultimate goal consists solely of one's own ego and desires.[1]

So how are we as Christians called to respond? Must we give in to these worldly pressures? Consider the crucial advice St. Paul gave to the Christians living in pagan Rome: "Do not be conformed to this world but be transformed by the renewal of your mind, that you may prove what is the will of God, what is good and acceptable and perfect" (Rom 12:2).

Just like these early Christians in Rome, we must resist being "conformed to this world." Much of what we absorb from our secular culture — about love, success, beauty, happiness, what is right and wrong — not only excludes the light of faith but often undermines what Jesus reveals about these important matters. If we're not careful, we might find ourselves trusting in the "wisdom" of the world more than the truth Jesus revealed: "It's not hurting anyone." "Everyone does it." "It's okay if we truly love each other." "That's not right for me personally." "It's just a movie."

As disciples, we are called to live in the truth. Instead of giving in to the various philosophies of our day, instead of allowing the world to tell us what to think, instead of "going with the flow" of popular opinion, Jesus invites us to "renew our minds." And this is not simply an academic matter; it has profound implications for our lives. What

Notes

I am the way, the truth and the life.

— *John 14:6*

we believe about life — who we are, what we are made for, what love is, how to be happy — molds us and shapes us. Living in the truth makes us happy and fulfilled. Indeed, the truth sets us free (Jn 8:32).

─────────────── **DISCUSS** ───────────────

How have you been tempted to buy into the world's ideas about love, success, beauty, happiness or right and wrong? How can you battle against being "conformed to this world"?

───────────────────────────────────────

Do not be conformed to this world but be transformed by the renewal of your mind.

— Romans 12:2

RENEWING OUR MINDS

Considering the dangers we face in being conformed to this world, how can we take St. Paul's advice and "be transformed by the renewal of [our] minds"? Many ways are available to us. Let's look at three that are the most foundational for any disciple of Jesus.

● *Scripture*

First, a disciple renews his mind through regular reading of Scripture. The Bible is no ordinary book: It's inspired by God. It is God's Word in the language of men. Those divine words written thousands of years ago reach across the centuries to continue to touch people's hearts and minds today. When we read the Bible, we aren't reading an old, irrelevant text; we are encountering God speaking to us — personally, in this moment. Consider what the Church, Scripture, and the saints teach about the power of the Bible in our lives:

> "For in the sacred books, the Father who is in heaven meets his children with great love and speaks with them."[2]

> "For the word of God is living and active, sharper than any two-edged sword, piercing to the division

of soul and spirit, of joints and marrow, and discerning the thoughts and intentions of the heart." (Heb 4:12)

"Ignorance of Scripture is ignorance of Christ." (St. Jerome)

Reading Scripture every day is a vital way to form yourself in the mind of Christ.

Church Teaching

Second, a disciple renews his mind by encountering what Jesus teaches through the Catholic Church. As the God who became man, Jesus Christ is the fullness of God's revelation; he entrusted this revelation to his closest friends, the apostles, who in turn entrusted it to their successors (the bishops) throughout the ages, so that all nations and all generations could know the truth and path to happiness (Mt 16:18–19; 18:18; 28:18–20).

What a tremendous gift Jesus has left us! And yet, do we take time to learn what Jesus is teaching us through the Catholic Church? A disciple makes formation in the Catholic Faith a priority. There are many good programs, retreats, books, and resources about the Catholic Faith. But one basic place to start is the *Catechism of the Catholic Church*, the official modern-day summary of what the apostles have passed on to us today. When we read the *Catechism*, we can be sure we are encountering the truth God has handed on through the Church.

What We Consume

Third, we must be careful about what we put into our minds: what we watch on screens, what we listen to, what we read, and what we look at. We are made in such a way that what we put into our minds changes us. It shapes how we look at reality and perceive what is good. It influences our desires and what we want to pursue in life. It's important for us to ask

ourselves: Does the media I take in reflect what is true, good, and beautiful? Or do I watch shows that fill my mind with a vision of life, beauty, love, and sexuality that is contrary to what Jesus teaches about these matters?

Being transformed by the renewal of our minds often means taking a hard look at what we take in and seriously asking ourselves whether it strengthens or hinders our view of reality. But it also means finding time to fill our minds with good things like the Bible and the *Catechism*. There are also many good and faithful Catholic books, resources, and devotional texts. By regularly taking in good Catholic content, our minds can slowly be conformed to the mind of Christ. That's why St. Paul exhorts us, "whatever is true, whatever is honorable, whatever is just, whatever is pure, whatever is lovely, whatever is gracious, if there is any excellence, if there is anything worthy of praise, think about these things" (Phil 4:8). Imagine how differently we would think and live if we put away some of the music, media, and shows that constantly affect our thoughts, desires and emotions and replaced those with images and words that elevated our minds to consider the things of God.

—————————————— **DISCUSS** ——————————————

Based on the recommendations in this section, what content do you need to make more a part of your life to form your mind well? What might you need to limit or get rid of?

TAKE ACTION

First, take a little time for reflection:

- How has worldly thinking creeped into my life?

- Am I thinking with the mind of Christ?

- Do I know what Christ teaches, and why?

- Am I being shaped by things that are true, good, and beautiful?

- Am I consuming media that is leading me to think rightly about God, myself, and the world?

- Which teachings of the Church do I struggle to understand?

Next, plan on what steps you will take to form yourself in the truth of Jesus Christ:

- How can I incorporate Scripture and the teachings of the Church into my life?

- Which books will I begin reading?

- What shows or entertainment will I stop watching or listening to?

As you make these changes, remember to start small. You likely won't be successful if you try to commit yourself to reading 500 pages a day and listening to 20 Catholic podcasts. Instead, pick a couple key practices to add to your week and try to make those practices a habit.

KEY CONCEPTS

Romans 12:2: "Do not be conformed to this world but be transformed by the renewal of your mind, that you may prove what is the will of God, what is good and acceptable and perfect."

What we put into our minds changes us. It becomes a part of us, shaping how we look at reality and what we perceive as good and influencing our desires. This is why we want to make it a priority to form our minds with the Faith.

John 14:6: "I am the way, the truth and the life."

ADDITIONAL RESOURCES

Who Am I to Judge?: Responding to Relativism with Logic and Love by Dr. Edward Sri

Bible Basics for Catholics: A New Picture of Salvation History by John Bergsma

The Real Story by Edward Sri and Curtis Martin

Theology for Beginners by Frank Sheed

SLS20 Talk on focusequip.org: "Day 4 Keynote: The Teaching of the Apostles" by Dr. Jonathon Reyes

Notes

[1] Joseph Ratzinger, "Mass 'Pro Eligendo Romano Pontifice,' Homily of His Eminence Card. Joseph Ratzinger, Dean of the College of Cardinals," accessed February 25, 2020, Vatican.va.

[2] Vatican Council II, *Dei Verbum*, accessed February 25, 2020, Vatican.va, 21.

THE HIGH CALL
TO MISSION

MORAL
AUTHORITY

AND "THE
BIG 3"

Optional *Lectio Divina* Prayer

1. Read Matthew 5:13–16.
2. Meditate on the words.
3. Speak to Christ about this passage.
4. Rest and listen in God's presence.
5. Discuss together.

PART ONE: MORAL AUTHORITY AND CHRISTIAN LEADERSHIP   *Notes*

*Note: This article is divided into two parts: **Moral Authority and Christian Leadership** and **Moral Authority in Action: Living Out the Big 3**. It is meant to be broken up into two (or more) conversations.*

There was seemingly little reason for the world to know about Agnes Gonxha Bojaxhiu.

She was born into a middle-class home in the Ottoman Empire at the turn of the 20th century. She eventually moved to one of the poorest parts of the world and worked for decades in anonymity, caring for the destitute and tirelessly doing menial tasks that no one else was willing to do.

But slowly, news about her work started to spread. Women from other countries began to join her, and reporters started observing her life and writing about her amazing witness. Her work expanded to other countries, and people from around the world wanted to know more about her. In time, she became one of the most influential women of the 20th century.

In 1979, she received the Nobel Peace Prize. Upon accepting the award, she spoke to the crowd about the demands of real love, how God was the true source of peace and how abortion was the greatest destroyer of peace today. Everyone cheered, even though the crowd had many people in it who did not hold these Christian ideals.

In 1982, she gave the commencement address at Harvard. She received a standing ovation for a speech in which she told young people to embrace chastity and the dignity of all life. How was such a countercultural message received so well at a secular university like Harvard?

Acts speak louder than words; let your words speak and your actions teach.

— *St. Anthony of Padua*

The ways of the Lord are not easy, but we were not created for an easy life, but for great things, for goodness.

— *Pope Benedict XVI*

In 1985, the United Nations honored her at its 40th anniversary celebration, and she spoke before the most powerful leaders in the world. In her speech, she told the crowd that they were children of God and that they needed to pray because they couldn't give what they didn't have. More applause followed — the United Nations was praising a religious message!

General Perez de Cuellar, Secretary of the United Nations at the time, said this when introducing her:

> This is a hall of words. A few days ago we had, in this rostrum, the most powerful men in the world. Now we have the privilege to have the most powerful woman in the world. I don't think I need to present her. She doesn't need words. She does need deeds. ... She is the United Nations. She is peace in this world.[1]

Who is this woman whom the United Nations called "the most powerful woman in the world"? And what made her so powerful? Agnes Gonxha Bojaxhiu is now known as St. Mother Teresa of Calcutta. She became one of the most influential leaders in the world — not because of wealth, or fame, or any title or position she held, but because of the remarkable way she lived her life.

—————————————— **DISCUSS** ——————————————

What was it about Mother Teresa that made people want to follow her and listen to what she had to say? How was her kind of leadership and influence different from what people commonly think about leadership today?

WHAT IS MORAL AUTHORITY?

Some people influence the world through their riches, fame, or positions of power. Mother Teresa, however, exhibited a very different kind of authority, one that's much more influential, modeled by Christ himself. It's the kind of authority to which any ordinary person can aspire. She had what can be called "moral authority."

Moral authority is the ability to lead others not by our title or position, but by the way we live. In leadership, far more important than one's personality, talents, titles, or techniques is one's moral character. Jesus wasn't an effective leader because he held great titles or offices in the first-century Jewish world. He didn't seek to make a name for himself or build a platform. It was his humility, his courage, his love, his entire way of life that inspired thousands to follow him, and that left a deep and lasting impression on more than a billion people throughout the world to this day.

Jesus' example challenges us to ask ourselves what kind of leader we want to be. Are we striving to live outstanding lives like Christ, to pursue heroic virtue, to give God and the people in our lives the very best of ourselves, like Christ did? St. Mother Teresa made many sacrifices and gave her all to serve the poorest of the poor around the world. Her actions spoke much louder than her words. Her amazing witness of sacrificial love inspired many people to live a little more like her and listen to her message. That's the influence of someone who has moral authority.

───────────────── **DISCUSS** ─────────────────

When have you witnessed moral authority (or a lack thereof) in your own life? What are the benefits of leading with moral authority?

──

CHRISTIAN LEADERSHIP

All this is especially true for anyone stepping into Christian leadership. Because Christian leaders represent so noble a King,

they must strive to live beautiful, noble lives, reflecting what Jesus taught and participating deeply in Christ's life. The more our lives are conformed to Christ, guided by Christ, animated by Christ, the more our leadership will bear fruit. As St. Paul says, "it is no longer I who live, but Christ who lives in me" (Gal 2:20).

Our leadership, however, will not be effective if we are not firmly rooted in Christ's way of life. We are less likely to inspire others to daily prayer, for example, if we ourselves don't have a daily prayer life. We won't be effective in inviting people to follow Jesus if we ourselves don't follow his moral teachings in a certain area. We can't give what we don't have. Even more dangerous is living contrary to Christ's teachings, which completely undermines our leadership. We must go above and beyond, living beyond reproach, so that there is no question as to whether we are living a life of moral integrity. Because Christian leaders represent Christ, they will be held to a higher standard in the way they live. According to James 3:1, "Teachers ... shall be judged with greater strictness."

Let's be clear. Moral authority is about much more than making sure we "practice what we preach." And even less is it a tactic for gaining worldly respect. We must realize there's a profound *spiritual* principle at work here: To the extent we are living deeply in Christ, living according to his plan — morally, spiritually, sacramentally — Jesus can work through us in amazing ways, in our families, friendships, workplaces, and mission. But if we are not rooted deeply in Christ and living fully according to his plan, our leadership will

We are affected more deeply toward God by a ten-minute visit with a saintly person than we are in ten years spent with a mediocre individual.

— *Thomas Dubay*

suffer. Christ will not work through us as powerfully as leaders. We become more of a roadblock to the Holy Spirit than his instrument.

Whether we become leaders on campus, in the workplace, in our parishes, or in our own homes, let's strive to be leaders with moral authority. As Thomas Dubay once wrote, "We are affected more deeply toward God by a ten-minute visit with a saintly person than we are in ten years spent with a mediocre individual."[2] Others are depending on us to live our lives well. Let's not settle to be mediocre people. Let's strive to be saints.

DISCUSS

Are you living as a faithful representative of Jesus? Is your life a witness to the Gospel? How might you need to grow to be a more compelling witness of Christ? What change can you make starting this week?

PART TWO: MORAL AUTHORITY IN ACTION: LIVING OUT THE BIG 3

*Note: This article is divided into two parts: **Moral Authority and Christian Leadership** and **Moral Authority in Action: Living Out the Big 3**. It is meant to be broken up into two (or more) conversations.*

THE BIG 3

Three key areas are particularly important for living with moral authority today: *chastity, sobriety,* and *excellence.* It's worth giving attention to these because it's especially challenging to live these virtues in our secular world, and when we fall in these areas, we become particularly enslaved. The world tries to promise us that we will find fulfillment in sex, drunkenness, substance abuse, distractions, and amusements that keep us from giving the best of ourselves; however, in each of these areas, the Lord desires for us to live in freedom rather than in slavery and shame. Not only does he want our own freedom, but he wants us to be models of this freedom for others. If we're not being intentional about living like Jesus — living beyond reproach — in these three areas, our ability to love others and to influence the world for Christ will be severely undermined.

As we dive into each of these three virtues, take time to pause and discuss after each one. Do not feel like you have to discuss all three of these in one sitting. The information and questions are meant to help you identify areas where you may need to grow and discern how the Lord might be inviting you to deeper healing and freedom so that you can be a more authentic witness of his life and love.

CHASTITY

The definition of love is "to will the good of another" (CCC 1766), to seek what's best for the other person. Jesus' teachings on chastity are all about equipping us to experience and give this kind of authentic, lasting love, which is the kind of love we long for. Our highly emotional and overly romantic culture, however, tends to confuse love with lust, which is focused on self — on what *I* get out of the other person or how I can use them for my own gratification.

Every day we are faced with many choices about whether to love or use others — in our thoughts, in our glances, in our physical actions. Jesus says in Matthew 5:27-28, "You have heard that it was said, 'You shall not commit adultery.' But I say to you that everyone who looks at a woman lustfully has already committed adultery with her in his heart."

In these verses, Jesus illustrates that chastity is about much more than simply avoiding sex outside of marriage. At its heart, chastity is about having the ability to love others the way God has called us to love: with a pure heart and mind, not as a slave to selfishness or lust. We do this in three important ways.

First, we must live purity in our *thoughts*. In a world filled with immodest images, pornography, sexting, hookup apps, and sexually explicit content, we must go out of our way to guard our eyes and maintain purity in mind and heart. Jesus says in Luke 6:45, "The good man out of the good treasure of his heart produces good, and the evil man out of his evil treasure produces evil."

Second, we also need to live out chastity in our *actions*. Sex is not just a physical act of pleasure: The physical union is meant to express a profound, personal union between husband and wife. In giving their bodies to each other in this most intimate union, spouses are giving their very selves to each other. Sex itself, and sexual actions leading up to sex, are intended by God for marriage. That's why premarital sex and any physical action that causes arousal in you or someone else (e.g., touching sexual body parts, mutual masturbation, oral sex, etc.) is immoral outside of marriage, for it is not oriented toward an act of *total* self-giving. The couple experiences pleasures that are particularly associated with sexual union apart from a total commitment to the other person.

Even within marriage, some sexual acts are not chaste, are not a total gift of self, if they are not open to life. Contraception, for example, prevents couples from fully giving themselves to each other as they hold back that which is most intimately theirs — their fertility — and attempt to have the pleasure of the sexual act without a total acceptance of the other person, including their fertility.

Third, to lead with moral authority in terms of chastity, we must also be careful not to cause scandal. For those who are not married, resting in the same bed, sleeping over at a boyfriend/girlfriend's house, or having imprudent one-on-one time late at night may not only be a temptation — a near occasion of sin — but it may also give others the wrong impression. For married couples, having too much alone time with someone of the opposite sex who is not their spouse can cause similar problems. A Christian leader does not merely avoid doing evil but is held to a higher standard (Jas 3:1). They must live beyond reproach and avoid doing anything that could give the impression of immoral behavior.

Notes

Finally, pursuing chastity in our thoughts and in our actions, including how our actions could be perceived, is not just about avoiding a long list of sinful actions. It is truly about conforming ourselves to Christ and learning to love through a total gift of self, just as Christ does for us. In the words of the *Catechism*, when "man governs his passions" he "finds peace" (CCC 2339). In spite of what the world often tell us — that enjoying the pleasures of sex whenever we desire is necessary for love and happiness — a life of chastity allows us instead to use our sexuality in a way that brings the authentic love, joy, freedom, and peace for which we long.

DISCUSS

It can be helpful to take an honest look at where we are in regard to chastity and to bring the challenges we face to light. Were there any specific areas of sexuality mentioned here that have been a challenge for you? How might the Lord be inviting you to break old habits, to grow in virtue, or to seek healing?

SOBRIETY

Sobriety is the exercise of the virtue of temperance (self-control) when it comes to alcohol, drugs, and other substances. When of legal age, there is nothing wrong with drinking alcohol in moderation;

Jesus' first miracle involved changing water into wine for a wedding feast. Still, St. Peter cautions us to stay alert: "Be sober, be watchful. Your adversary the devil prowls around like a roaring lion, seeking someone to devour" (1 Pt 5:8).

Some might wonder, "Why is drunkenness or losing sobriety on drugs such a problem? What's wrong with it?" Getting drunk or being high on drugs like marijuana impairs our reason and therefore makes it harder for us to make good, free, deliberate choices and live virtuously. When we drink in excess, for example, we intentionally inhibit our intellect and lose control of that which is most intimately ours — our free will — and we give the devil an opportunity to wreak havoc, setting us up to make other bad decisions that can harm ourselves and others. As a result, St. Paul lists drunkenness as one of the sins that keeps a person from the kingdom of God (Gal 5:21). St. Thomas Aquinas explained that drunkenness is a grave sin because it breaks our relationship with God.

As with chastity, to lead with moral authority in terms of sobriety, we must not merely avoid drunkenness. We must also be careful not to cause scandal by being too closely associated with drunkenness taking place around us. Jesus loved everyone and reached out to people of all backgrounds, even sinners. He was known for having meals with drunkards and prostitutes. But we never read about Jesus hanging out with prostitutes at a brothel while they were seducing their men or having drinks with drunkards during their group drinking binges. Our presence in certain settings might give the impression that we are okay with the sinful activity or, even worse, that we ourselves participate in it. When Pope St. John Paul II once explained the proper balance in his own ministry of accompaniment, he said God called him "to live with people, everywhere to be with them, in everything but sin."[2] This should be our goal as well.

There are a few questions you can ask yourself to gauge your relationship with drugs or alcohol: Am I drinking underage, in violation of Paul's command to respect the law (Rom 13:1–7)? In social settings, am I more focused on the alcohol than the people

Notes

Chastity is a triumphant affirmation of love.

— *St. Josemaría Escrivá*

around me? Are alcohol or drugs causing other problems in my life or in my relationships? Do I need additional help in overcoming an addiction? Are my actions with regard to alcohol or drugs leading others into sin? If you answered yes to any of these questions, then it might be time to evaluate your relationship with alcohol or drugs and consider if the Lord might be inviting you to greater freedom through sobriety.

Finally, sobriety allows you to be truly free in the most important areas of your life. Properly using alcohol and avoiding drug use allows you to keep custody over your decisions while also allowing you to celebrate appropriately in situations where it is customary to enjoy alcohol. Sobriety is not about limiting your freedom but rather about allowing you to embrace true freedom and not be dependent on any substance for fun, friendship, or fellowship with others. When we fully possess ourselves and aren't slaves to substances, we can enter more deeply into the relationships that mean the most to us: our relationships with God, our families, our friends, and our community.

DISCUSS

Take a moment and discuss the role of alcohol and drugs in your life. Do you struggle to remain sober with these substances? How do they affect your life? Are you getting drunk, drinking underage, or giving too much attention to alcohol? How are you practicing the virtue of sobriety, and how do you still need to grow?

EXCELLENCE

Excellence is the ability to give the best of ourselves in our vocation and daily responsibilities. The person committed to excellence does not settle for mediocrity, especially in the things that matter most in life. For married couples, this means striving to be the best spouse or parent they can be. For students, this means giving their finest effort in their studies. In the workplace, with whatever jobs, tasks, or projects are entrusted to us, we should always seek to give the best of ourselves, realizing that we are ultimately serving Jesus in these endeavors. As St. Paul wrote, "Whatever your task, work heartily, as serving the Lord and not men, knowing that from the Lord you will receive the inheritance as your reward; you are serving the Lord Christ" (Col 3:23–24).

The pursuit of excellence also challenges us to reflect on how we use our time, including our down time. Do we spend a lot of time playing video games, watching television, browsing social media, binging on Netflix, looking at our phones, or wasting time on YouTube? While there's nothing wrong with moderate use of these media, these passive forms of entertainment weaken our will and character when we use them habitually. The amount of time spent in these activities greatly affects your ability to give the best of yourself to others and do great things with your life. If you don't intentionally practice self-control in these areas, you will develop habits that makes it difficult for you to give the best of yourself — the best of your time, attention, love, and sacrifice — to your work, your spouse, your children, and your friends. Are you training your will to deny yourself, make sacrifices, take on challenges, and persevere through difficult tasks? Or are you training your will to prefer being passively entertained and your mind to be constantly distracted? Do you fill your mind more with the true, the good, and the beautiful or with frivolous amusements and images that drag you down? Are you intentionally setting parameters around how much time you spend on your phone, on social media, or on screens watching shows? If you are not intentionally practicing a little bit of self-denial in these areas, you are likely becoming gradually enslaved by them.

As Christians, we should be pursuing excellence in every area of our lives.

We must also be careful not to allow our pursuit of excellence to turn into perfectionism, which is a distorted sense of excellence. It often involves having unrealistically high standards, an inordinate desire for achievement, and overcommitment. Perfectionism doesn't originate from true piety, from a desire to give God our best, but from insecurity: the fear of failure or rejection, the need to please others, a sense of self-reliance, or the belief that we need to earn God's love, which we know is not true.

Finally, when we live excellence in all the areas where God is calling us to serve — our families, our work, our studies, our downtime, our commitment to the Church and our community — we cooperate with him to build the kingdom of God. These aren't "extra" aspects of life that don't affect our relationship with God. Rather, they are the important settings he wants to use to mold us, shape us, and draw us closer to himself.

DISCUSS

Are there any areas of your life where you are struggling to live excellence (spiritual life, relationships, family/vocation, job/ education, health)? Are you struggling with perfectionism? If so, why? What would it look like for you to be excellent in the area in which you are struggling the most right now?

TAKE ACTION

Oftentimes, sins against the Big 3 become habits, and sometimes they have been habits in our lives for a very long time. But Jesus can triumph over any habit, wound, or addiction. You may not overcome these sins overnight, but with Christ, growth and healing are possible!

After you have identified any areas of the Big 3 that are holding you back from the life and leadership Christ is calling you to live, make a plan to begin building habits of virtue using the practical steps below:

- **Prayer and Sacraments.** We can't overcome our sins by ourselves. We need the help of God's grace to strengthen us in virtue and holiness.

- **Accountability.** To help you grow in virtue and root out sins in the areas of the Big 3, develop a plan for avoiding temptations and pursuing healthy behaviors, and then discuss it with an accountability partner who can support you and help hold you accountable to your plan.

- **Seeking Additional Help.** Sometimes our struggle with chastity, sobriety, or excellence requires more attention than what our accountability partner can provide. There's no shame in admitting that you need additional help; consider joining a support group or seeking out a professional.

KEY CONCEPTS

Moral Authority: The ability to influence others by the way we live, not by the position or title we hold

The Big 3: To have and lead with moral authority in today's culture, we especially need to live out chastity, sobriety, and excellence.

ADDITIONAL RESOURCES:

True Leadership by the Harbinger Institute for Catholic Leadership, Ch. 6: "The Second Foundation — Character: Who am I?"

From focusequip.org: Path to Freedom (For Men) or Uncompromising Purity (For Women)

From the FOCUS Blog on focusequip.org: Cultural Apologetics series — see specifically these features:

- "Sex and Sanctity: A Discussion of Sex Before Marriage" by Jason Evert
- "Porn and Relationships: A Discussion of the Problem of Porn" by Matt Fradd
- "The Pill: No Small Matter: A Discussion about Contraception" by Dr. Janet Smith
- "A Catholic Approach to Alcohol: A Discussion of the Virtuous Use of Alcohol" by Dr. Jared Staudt

Men, Women, and the Mystery of Love by Dr. Edward Sri

CCC 2337–2359: "The Vocation to Chastity"

CCC 1803–1832: "The Virtues"

Notes

Notes

[1] Servants of the Pierced Hearts of Jesus and Mary, "Blessed Mother Teresa's Address to the United Nations on the Occasion of its 40th Anniversary," Piercedhearts.org, accessed March 4, 2020, https://www.piercedhearts.org/purity_heart_morality/mother_teresa_address_united_nations.htm.

[2] Thomas Dubay, "...*And You Are Christ's*" (San Francisco: Ignatius Press, 1987), 121.

[3] George Weigel, *Witness to Hope* (New York: Harper Perennial, 2005), 104.

FAITHFULNESS TO CHRIST AND HIS CHURCH

Optional *Lectio Divina* Prayer

1. Read John 6:53–69.
2. Meditate on the words.
3. Speak to Christ about this passage.
4. Rest and listen in God's presence.
5. Discuss together.

Do you know St. Peter's most heroic moment?

It wasn't when he dropped his fishing nets to follow Jesus. It wasn't when he recognized Jesus as the Messiah and received the keys to the kingdom. Arguably, it came in a lesser-known scene when Jesus taught something controversial that turned his popular public ministry upside down.

The enthusiastic crowds had been asking Jesus for a miraculous sign, like the manna that Moses provided for the Israelites in the desert. In response, Jesus told them about a greater food he would offer them: his own Body and Blood in the Eucharist. "Truly, truly, I say to you, unless you eat the flesh of the Son of man and drink his blood, you have no life in you; he who eats my flesh and drinks my blood has eternal life, and I will raise him up at the last day" (Jn 6:53–54).

But this teaching on the Eucharist was too much for their minds to grasp. Many in the crowds rejected Jesus at this moment, saying, "How can this man give us his flesh to eat?" (Jn 6:52). Even his own disciples struggled, saying, "This is a hard saying, who can listen to it?" (Jn 6:60). Some of those disciples rejected Jesus and walked away that day.

Turning to the Twelve Apostles, Jesus said, "Will you also go away?"

That's when Peter's heroic moment came into play. He responds, saying, "Lord, to whom shall we go? You have the words of eternal life; and we have believed and have come to know that you are the Holy One of God" (Jn 6:68–69).

Notice that Peter doesn't say, "Jesus, I'll follow you because this teaching makes perfect sense to me." Peter is probably just as puzzled as everyone else. But the difference between Peter and the crowds is that he trusts Jesus and stays with him, whereas the others walk away.

---------------------------- **DISCUSS** ----------------------------

What stands out to you about Peter's response? What does this teach you about following Jesus?

LEADING BY FAITH

When we are in a position of Christian leadership, we are not asking people to follow us, but rather the one true leader, Jesus Christ. And that comes with a tremendous responsibility — for our teaching is not our own. We are heralds of the Gospel, "ambassadors for Christ" (2 Cor 5:20), witnesses to the truth he revealed. As representatives of so noble a King, we must be careful to faithfully pass on the truth that Jesus revealed — and to never, under any condition, pass on ideas that are contrary to the teachings of his Church.

After all, Jesus himself established the Church so that people throughout the ages could come to know him and his plan for our lives. That's why he gave authority to his apostles to teach in his name. He said to them, "He who hears you hears me, and he who rejects you rejects me, and he who rejects me rejects him who sent me" (Mt 10:40). That same authority was handed on to the apostles' successors, the bishops, throughout the centuries to today.

Take a moment right now and feel the weight of what this means: To accept the teachings of the apostles is to accept Jesus. To the extent we knowingly reject the teachings of the apostles (and their successors), we are also distancing ourselves from Jesus. That's why it's absolutely crucial for Christian leaders to represent Jesus faithfully, to guard the "deposit of faith" — not to pass on a "counterfeit faith" based on our own opinions or the popular whims of the world (2 Tm 3:8), but rather the true faith of Jesus and the Catholic Church.

This won't always be easy. Jesus himself regularly experienced disagreement and opposition to his teaching. We live in a world that often doesn't accept God's truth about human life, love, sex, marriage, the poor, and the dignity of every human person no matter their age, race, religion, or beliefs. This leads us to a choice: When Christ's teaching is unpopular or, worse still, labeled as old-fashioned, impossible, judgmental, or even evil, will we stand up for the truth? Or will we deny our Lord Jesus Christ?

St. Paul warned about times not unlike our own. He emphasized that the most important thing Christian leaders can do in an era of doctrinal and moral confusion is to be steady and grounded in faithfully passing on the truth:

> [P]reach the word, be urgent in season and out of season ... For the time is coming when people will not endure sound teaching, but having itching ears they will accumulate for themselves teachers to suit their own likings, and will turn away from listening to the truth and wander into myths. As for you, always be steady ... do the work of an evangelist, fulfil your ministry. (2 Tm 4:2–5)

In sum, we can't be "cafeteria Catholics." When we eat a meal in a cafeteria, we can pick and choose which food we want to put on our plate. But we can't do that with the teachings of Christ and his Church; we can't pick and choose which Catholic teachings we want to follow and pass on to others and which ones we don't. Our teaching is not our own. We represent Christ. Even when these

Notes

He who hears you hears me, and he who rejects you rejects me, and he who rejects me rejects him who sent me.

— Luke 10:16

teachings challenge us or when the world around us rejects them, we need to be faithful to Jesus.

──────────────── **DISCUSS** ────────────────

Have you ever thought of yourself as a representative of Jesus? Have you embraced that responsibility by accepting the teachings of Jesus and his Church? How have you seen Jesus' teaching come into conflict with the ideas and opinions of the world?

DIFFICULTIES VS. DOUBTS

But what if we still have some questions about the Catholic Faith, whether it be related to the Church's teaching about the Immaculate Conception of Mary, the real presence of Jesus in the Eucharist, contraception, same-sex marriage, or the preferential love Christians must have for the poor? Can we still be Jesus' followers, faithful representatives of him and his Church?

Here, we need to understand the difference between having a difficulty and having a doubt.

Ten thousand difficulties do not make one doubt.

— St. John Henry Cardinal Newman

Difficulties are the challenges that we have in understanding a particular aspect of the Catholic Faith. When we face questions about a certain Catholic teaching, a part of us wonders, "Is this right? Could this be true?" But at the same time, we still trust Jesus and the Church more than ourselves, so we're willing to accept it. Like Peter when he was confronted with Christ's mind-blowing teaching about the Eucharist, we may not fully understand an aspect of the Catholic Faith, but we still believe it because we believe in Jesus and trust his Church. If Jesus were standing before us when we have these difficulties, we, too, would say, "Lord, to whom shall we go? You have the words of eternal life; and we have believed and have come to know that you are the Holy One of God" (Jn 6:68–69). As St. John Henry Cardinal Newman once said: "Ten thousand difficulties do not make one doubt" (CCC 157).

Doubt, however, is something different. It's ultimately a lack of trust in Jesus and the Church he established. When someone doubts, they withhold belief, refusing to believe what has been revealed — like "Doubting Thomas," the apostle who for a week refused to believe in the risen Christ, or the crowds who rejected Jesus' teaching about the Eucharist and walked away from him. When we oppose the teachings of Jesus as handed down through the Catholic Church, we undermine our role as Christians. We are not true ambassadors of Jesus. We present our own ideas as being wiser than what Jesus taught and do great harm in misleading the people we serve.

Notes

DISCUSS

Do you have any difficulties or doubts? Are there any teachings of the Church that you struggle with? How can you grow toward embracing those teachings wholeheartedly?

GROWING IN FAITH

Though we may wrestle with difficulties, there is a way forward. Faith is not a blind acceptance of what we do not understand; instead, a believer should *seek understanding*. According to the Catechism: "it is intrinsic to faith that a believer desires to know better the one in whom he has put his faith and to understand what he has revealed; a more penetrating knowledge will in turn call forth a greater faith, increasingly set afire by love" (CCC 158). St. Augustine described this well when he professed, "I believe, in order to understand; and I understand, the better to believe" (CCC 158). Deepening our understanding does not limit our freedom, but rather allows our "yes" to be truly free.

As you prepare to serve as a leader for Christ and grow in your understanding of the Faith, a great way to reaffirm and deepen your belief in Jesus and the teachings of the Church is to recite a traditional prayer called the "Act of Faith." Whether you are solid in your convictions about the Catholic Faith or you have questions about certain teachings, the Act of Faith helps you to declare your

faith in God and your willingness to trust that the Church teaches the truth. Many saints and ordinary Christians have found strength in making an Act of Faith like this:

> O my God, I firmly believe that you are one God in three divine persons, Father, Son and Holy Spirit. I believe that your divine Son became man and died for our sins, and that he will come to judge the living and the dead. I believe these and all the truths which the holy Catholic Church teaches, because in revealing them you can neither deceive nor be deceived. Amen.

--- **DISCUSS** ---

Do you want to say an Act of Faith right now as a profession of total faith in Jesus and his Church?

TAKE ACTION

If you currently doubt certain teachings of the Church, it's time to discuss those things. If you already accept all the teachings of Jesus and his Church, take a moment and consider some of the teachings you don't understand well.

Make two lists. For the first, write out some teachings you don't understand or have a hard time believing. For the second, consider some teachings you believe but would have trouble explaining to someone else who was confused about them.

Notes

Then, make a plan. How can you grow in your understanding of these teachings?

KEY CONCEPTS

Apostolic Authority: Jesus gave his apostles authority to teach: "He who hears you hears me, and he who rejects you rejects me, and he who rejects me rejects him who sent me" (Lk 10:16). That same authority was handed on to the apostles' successors, the bishops, throughout the centuries to today.

Ambassadors for Christ: As members of the kingdom, we are representatives of the King and must faithfully bear witness to his teachings (2 Cor 5:20).

Difficulties vs. Doubts: Difficulties are the challenges that we have in understanding a particular aspect of the Catholic Faith. Doubts show a lack of trust in Jesus and the Church he established.

ADDITIONAL RESOURCES:

Why We're Catholic by Trent Horn

CCC 142–165: "I Believe"

CCC 74–95: "The Transmission of Divine Revelation"

Fides et Ratio by Pope St. John Paul II

SLS20 Talk on focusequip.org: "Leading from a Catholic Worldview" by Helen Alvaré

THE HIGH CALL

TO MISSION

Optional *Lectio Divina* Prayer

1. Read Matthew 9:35–38.
2. Meditate on the words.
3. Speak to Christ about this passage.
4. Rest and listen in God's presence.
5. Discuss together.

The most important battle you will ever fight is not in business, politics, or a military campaign.

It all has to do with what role you choose to play in the struggle that has been raging since the beginning of time. It's the battle between God and the devil, good and evil, heaven and hell — either loving God even to the point of contempt for self or loving self to the point of contempt for God.[1] This is the battle happening within every human heart, regardless of whether we consciously realize it, and it has eternal consequences.

This is the crucial question many saints challenge us to face. St. Ignatius of Loyola, the founder of the Jesuits and author of the renowned *Spiritual Exercises,* invites us to consider the real spiritual battle taking place around us at every moment. St. Ignatius' famous "Meditation on the Two Standards" reveals the choice that every person of faith must make: For which side of the battle will I give my life?[2]

Put yourself in the scene. Two commanders stand on opposing battlefields, calling on soldiers to follow them. On one side, a riotous, angry crowd presses in around their general, who sits atop a chair of smoke and fire, terrifying in shape and even more horrible in demeanor. He charges his troops to scatter from the field, "not omitting any provinces, places, states, nor any persons," and to use their "nets and chains" to entice souls away from the love of God and get them to give their lives to pleasure, possessions, power, and pride.

At the other end of the battlefield stands another Commander-in-Chief, beautiful and full of love. He looks out over "all his servants and friends." They are generous, courageous, and ready to make many sacrifices to serve the Lord. Seeing the destruction and despair being spread by the rival army, Jesus, the "Lord of all the world chooses so many persons — apostles, disciples, etc. — and sends them through all the world, spreading his sacred doctrine."[3]

It is a call to mission. Jesus sends them out to bring souls to his love. He calls for people to give their whole lives for the kingdom of God and for the love of souls — souls who, if there is no one willing to go out to them with the Gospel, will be swept away by the enemy. Our knowledge of what Christ has done for us and our love for others should propel us to action: Who will say "Yes" to Christ's call? Jesus waits under his raised standard to see who will come to him.

This is where you come in. What will *you* do? Which camp will you serve? Where will you dwell? These are the questions St. Ignatius challenges us to ask. It is up to us to choose which banner and which army we will claim as our own.

—————————————— **DISCUSS** ——————————————

What stands out to you in this meditation? Where is the Lord directing your attention?

_____

AN URGENT INVITATION

This meditation should awaken in us the urgency to share Christ's love with others. As Christians, we don't believe in reincarnation; no one gets a "do-over," a second chance to help people in some second, third, or fourth life. No, the time is now. This generation of Christians is responsible for helping this generation of souls. Today, people suffer from all kinds of poverty: material poverty and slavery, social poverty, psychological poverty, poverty of relationships and the poverty of being unknown, unloved, and forgotten. Most of all, there is a particular urgency to serve those in need spiritually — to reach souls who do not know Christ and have not surrendered their lives to him, souls who may be forever separated from God unless Christians go out to them and share the Gospel.

You might be thinking, "I can see that this battle is real. But what does it have to do with me? What good could I do?" The truth is this: Jesus invites you to participate in his mission to save the world. He has people whom he specifically desires for you to encounter, accompany, and love. He does not expect you to be perfectly ready, but he does invite you to give him your small and humble "yes" to his mission.

It can be tempting to sit on the sidelines, to believe that "somebody else will do it" and respond to the call in our place. But to abstain from the battle is not a neutral decision. It actually falls into the strategy of the devil's army. He celebrates when Christians choose not to give their lives to extending Christ's kingdom on earth — because that means there is less resistance in the world to his evil ways and fewer heralds of the Gospel, which means more souls may never come to know Christ's love and his eternal salvation.

—————————————— **DISCUSS** ——————————————

What do you think of this call to enter the battle of bringing souls to Christ? Does it intimidate you or inspire you? Where do you see your place in this battle for eternity?

THE INVITATION TO MISSION

Ignatius' powerful meditation is a clear call to action. People are dying each day, and their eternity hangs in the balance. How do we move from recognizing this call to Christ's mission toward beginning to live it in the world? The rest of this article traces the journey from accepting Christ's standard as your own to going out on mission for the salvation of souls. This can be broken down into three elements: the Message, the Mission, and the Method Modeled by the Master.

- The **Message**: *The Gospel and Your Story*

  As St. Ignatius' meditation shows, a spiritual battle is raging all around us, as Christ and his army fight for the salvation of all souls. Choosing to follow Christ and stand under his banner is the first step for entering the battle at his side. We cannot serve him in this battle if we are not totally committed to him, if we are not surrendered to him as Lord, if we do not allow him to reign over every aspect of our lives. We cannot serve him in this battle if we are not allowing ourselves to be transformed by the saving power of the cross. As you begin to think about Christ's mission, remember what God has done in your life and how he has redeemed you, healed you, and made you new.

DISCUSS

How has the decision to follow Christ changed or shaped your life? How are you continuing to grow in placing Christ at the center of your life?

- The **Mission**: *Missionary Discipleship*

  After coming to stand under Christ's banner, the next step for entering his mission is to receive the call. Like the invitation found in St. Ignatius' meditation, Jesus gave his disciples a very specific command in his last moments on Earth. Before he ascended into heaven, Jesus said to his disciples: 'All authority in heaven and on earth has been given to me. Go therefore and make disciples of all nations, baptizing them in the name of the Father and of the Son and of the Holy Spirit, teaching them to

Notes

observe all that I have commanded you; and lo, I am with you always, to the close of the age'" (Mt 28:18–20).

This is the mission Jesus entrusted to the Church, and he invites all of us who are baptized to participate in this work of evangelization as missionary disciples (cf. CCC 831). As Pope Francis says, "In virtue of their baptism, all the members of the People of God have become missionary disciples (cf. Mt 28:19). All the baptized, whatever their position in the Church or their level of instruction in the faith, are agents of evangelization."[4] It's not reserved for priests and religious or biblical scholars and missionaries. If we have truly encountered Christ, how can we not share him with others? "[I]t is unthinkable that a person should accept the Word and give himself to the kingdom without becoming a person who bears witness to it and proclaims it in his turn."[5] To the degree that we respond to this call, souls will be saved; to the degree that we fail to respond, souls will be lost. Our lack of commitment in evangelization can cost the eternal life of souls.

DISCUSS

What do you think of the fact that you could play a role in inviting others to choose the standard of Christ and receive eternal life with him? What does it mean to you that Christ would entrust you with such a mission?

- The **Method Modeled by the Master**: The "Little Way of Evangelization"

Once you have chosen to serve on the side of Christ and answered the call to participate in the Church's mission of evangelization, how do you begin to go out and live that reality? We only need to look to what Jesus himself did throughout his earthly life and follow his example.

Jesus' way of evangelization was not a big way, but a little way. He did not travel the world to preach the Gospel to everyone on earth himself. Rather, he invested deeply in a few whom he formed in the Gospel of the kingdom and trained them to go out and do the same for others. Though he preached to the masses on some occasions, he spent most of his time investing in his small group of disciples. He spent three years living with them, teaching them, and showing them how to preach, heal, and lead as he did (Mt 4:19, 5:1ff). Then, he sent them out to preach the Gospel themselves and "make disciples of all nations" (Mt 28:19). Jesus' approach to evangelization is what we call the "Little Way of Evangelization." It is the approach to evangelization that Jesus modeled for us, the "Method Modeled by the Master." We aspire to imitate the method of evangelization that Jesus himself exemplified.

Consider the potential impact of this approach. Imagine one person pursuing a deep, personal relationship with Jesus and desiring for others to know him. She starts intentionally investing in three others who also have a desire to know Jesus. As they grow together, each of these missionary disciples begin investing in friends of their own — three, six or more — who eventually go on to do the same, forming more and more missionary disciples with each new cycle of growth.

The effects begin slowly: For example, one missionary disciple who reaches three others makes four. If each of those three

If you become who you are meant to be, you will set the world on fire.

— St. Catherine of Siena

new disciples reaches three others, the total becomes thirteen. For illustration purposes, imagine if all continued to go ideally well — after seven cycles, the total number could reach nearly 1,000, and after 13 cycles, more than 500,000. At this rate, the entire world could be reached in just 22 cycles — that's within one lifetime of the original disciple! While human weakness and failure will always be present along the way, this model, while purely mathematical, still beautifully illustrates the potential effect one person can have in impacting the world!

But the main point is that you don't have to be a talented speaker, a social media guru with thousands of followers, or the most charismatic person in your community to become a missionary disciple who impacts the world. You need only to invest in a few, winning them to Christ, building them up as faithful disciples and sending them out to do the same. Think of this as the "Little Way of Evangelization": Just as St. Thérèse of Lisieux was able to accomplish great holiness through humility, prayer, and little acts of great love, you too, by humbly and generously investing in a few, can bear tremendous fruit as you participate in the Church's mission of evangelization. All it takes is a lifetime of love. When we imitate Jesus' model of evangelization, we are more likely to see a kind of "spiritual multiplication," in which the Gospel touches many more people's lives , more missionary disciples are likely to be raised up and many more souls can be rescued from the reign of the evil one and brought into the kingdom of God.

Notes

DISCUSS

What inspires you about the "Little Way of Evangelization" that Jesus models? Why do you think it is important for evangelization to occur through relationships and deep, personal investment?

THE COST OF BATTLE

It's clear that the rewards of this battle are great, but they are not without cost. Jesus himself tells us in Luke 9:23, "'If any man would come after me, let him deny himself and take up his cross daily and follow me." To follow Jesus as missionary disciples will mean making sacrifices — like denying ourselves certain comforts and personal control — so we can pour out our lives for the conversion of others. We will experience suffering in a new way as we contend with rejection, discouragement, and disappointment. We will have to rearrange our schedules to make more time to love others, to grow in our own formation, and to spend time in prayer. But when we prioritize holiness and mission in our lives, we can have an eternal impact. As St. Catherine of Siena once said, "If you become who you are meant to be, you will set the world on fire!"

Now, considering everything that has been discussed in this article, are you willing to move forward? Will you take the next step? Will you accept this High Call to Mission?

———————————————— **DISCUSS** ————————————————

Will you accept Jesus' call to make disciples by committing to investing deeply in a few and teaching them to do the same?

TAKE ACTION

If you desire to move forward in the journey of becoming a missionary disciple, set up a consistent time to begin meeting for regular training in mission. Use this time to begin walking together intentionally on mission, even as you continue to share life together and grow in the Christian habits you have been forming.

As you enter more deeply into a life lived on mission, revisit this article frequently! The High Call to Mission is not a one-time event. After you commit to living out this mission, take this article to prayer or discuss it again regularly to rekindle your conviction and be reminded of Jesus' call to you.

KEY CONCEPTS

Missionary Disciple: "In virtue of their baptism, all the members of the People of God have become missionary disciples (cf. Mt 28:19). All the baptized, whatever their position in the Church or their level of instruction in the faith, are agents of evangelization."[6]

The Little Way of Evangelization — The Method Modeled by the Master: Jesus' way of evangelization was not a big way, but a little way. He did not travel the world to preach the Gospel to everyone on earth himself. Rather, he invested deeply in a few whom he formed in the Gospel of the kingdom and trained them to go out and do the same. In so doing, he imparted both faithfulness and fruitfulness that transformed the world. We are called to imitate Christ and his method to reach the world.

Notes

[1] St. Augustine, *City of God,* trans. by Marcus Dods (New York: Modern Library, 1950), XVI.28.

[2] St. Ignatius of Loyola, "Meditation on the Two Standards," in *The Spiritual Exercises of St. Ignatius of Loyola,* accessed March 5, 2020, https://www.sacred-texts.com/chr/seil/seil22.htm.

[3] Ibid.

[4] Francis, *Evangelii Gaudium,* accessed November 3, 2020, Vatican.va, 120.

[5] Paul VI, *Evangelii Nuntiandi,* accessed March 5, 2020, Vatican.va, 24.

[6] Francis, *Evangelii Gaudium,* 120.

Notes

SEND

SEND
For the Leader

"Send" articles are designed to teach the vision, skills, and formation necessary to evangelize and accompany others effectively on the path of discipleship. Once someone has accepted the High Call to Mission, they need to be trained in how to do the work of evangelization and discipleship: "A serious preparation is needed for all workers of evangelization."[1] In the Send phase, there are two different types of articles: mission formation and personal formation. As you progress through this section, you do not need to lead these articles strictly in this order; feel free to share personal formation articles at some times and mission formation articles at other times, according to the needs and desires of those you are accompanying.

MISSION FORMATION

Mission formation articles are designed to give leaders the vision and skills they need to evangelize effectively.

PERSONAL FORMATION

Personal formation articles help leaders continue to deepen their relationship with Jesus and strengthen their Christian witness.

Notes

[1] Paul VI, *Evangelii Nuntiandi*, accessed May 25, 2020, Vatican.va, 73.

Notes

Notes

MISSION FORMATION

A
VISION FOR
MISSIONARY
DISCIPLESHIP

WIN
BUILD
SEND

Optional *Lectio Divina* Prayer

1. Read John 1:35-42.
2. Meditate on the words.
3. Speak to Christ about this passage.
4. Rest and listen in God's presence.
5. Discuss together.

PART ONE: WIN-BUILD-SEND

*Note: This article is divided into two parts: **Win-Build-Send** and **The Three Habits of Missionary Disciples**. It is meant to be broken up into two (or more) conversations.*

I n the early 1500s, two college students, Peter and Francis, were rooming together at the University of Paris.

The University was filled with all sorts of vices — brawling, drunkenness, and sexual immorality — among both students and their teachers. Peter and Francis both stayed out of this trouble, but more out of fear than piety. Francis hoped to use his nobility to live a posh lifestyle in luxury and comfort. Peter, however, could not quite decide what he wanted to do. At times he wanted to get married and become a lawyer, a teacher, or a physician; at other times, he wanted to become a simple priest or monk.

For three years, Francis and Peter continued to room together, until one day, their lives were completely changed. A thirty-six-year-old man named Ignatius became their new roommate. Ignatius had already lived a storied life. He began his young career in pursuit of worldly fame and fortune through military conquest; however, a cannonball to the leg left him bedridden for months. With nothing but time on his hands, Ignatius turned to the only books available to him: the Bible and a book on the lives of the saints. Reading these books led to a conversion experience, and Ignatius devoted his life completely to serving God.

Peter, like many other students, was quickly moved by Ignatius and soon shared his desire to win souls for Jesus Christ. He became a follower of Ignatius' way of life and wished to join his order. Francis, on the other hand, was quick to make fun of Ignatius and Peter.

For three years, Ignatius invested in Francis. He showed a deep interest in everything Francis did. Ignatius attended Francis' lectures, found Francis students to teach and even supplied him with money. You can imagine all the time they spent together as roommates: studying for classes, sharing meals, having discussions late into the night, and taking excursions around town. And yet, Francis was still resistant to Ignatius' invitations for him to go deeper in his faith.

At one point, Peter left the university on vacation, leaving Francis and Ignatius together. When Peter came back, his roommate of six years had changed. Francis had finally heeded Ignatius' question, "What profits a man to gain the whole world, if only to lose his soul?" (cf. Mk 8:36).

Soon, the three friends co-founded a new order: the Society of Jesus, also known as the Jesuits. Ignatius, whom we know now as St. Ignatius of Loyola, served as the superior general. Peter, now known as St. Peter Favre, went on to evangelize in Germany, Spain, and Portugal. And Francis, better known today as St. Francis Xavier, was sent to India as a missionary. He baptized hundreds of thousands in Asia and was, by most accounts, the greatest singular missionary force since St. Paul.

DISCUSS

What stands out to you about the way that Ignatius evangelized Peter and Francis? What does this story teach us about evangelization?

THE METHOD MODELED BY THE MASTER: WIN-BUILD-SEND

In St. Ignatius, we observe a great example of missionary discipleship. Francis was transformed from a worldly man to an otherworldly saint. But how can you and I accomplish this same work? How can we help form others who both know Jesus Christ and share him with the world?

PRAYER & ACCOMPANIMENT CHART

WIN

Winning through authentic friendship
- 1 Thes 2:8

Accept the Gospel
(Jn 17:3)

BUILD

Building in divine intimacy
- Acts 2:42

Accept the High Call to Mission
(Mt 28:18-20)

SEND

Sending with clarity and conviction for the Little Way of Evangelization
- 2 Tim 2:2, Jn 15:8

PROCESS OF EVANGELIZATION

"Above all the Gospel must be proclaimed. by witness." — EN 21

"There is no true evangelization if the name, the teaching, the life, the promises, the kingdom and the mystery of Jesus of Nazareth, the Son of God, are not proclaimed." — EN 22

"Proclamation only reaches full development when it is listened to, accepted and assimilated, and when it arouses a genuine adherence in the one who has thus received it." — EN 23

"It is unthinkable that a person should accept the Word and give himself to the kingdom without becoming a person who bears witness to it and proclaims it in his turn." — EN 24

"A serious preparation is needed for all workers of evangelization." — EN 73

The Church identifies three general phases in the process of someone's journey as a missionary disciple, phrases we simply call Win, Build, and Send. These phases are separated by two key moments: saying yes to Jesus and the Gospel, and accepting the High Call to Mission. As we seek to form missionary disciples, each of these phases has its own goals and objectives. Let's look at these key phases and learn how we can accompany others in becoming missionary disciples.

Note: As you read this section, please refer to the Prayer and Accompaniment chart on the previous page, which provides a visual representation of this path of missionary discipleship. This tool will be discussed in various articles throughout this "Send" section of articles as a tool for praying for others and walking with them in mission.

Win

The first step to forming missionary disciples is to lead people to a conversion, to a life-shaping encounter with Jesus Christ — one in which they turn away from sin, surrender their lives to Jesus as Lord, and follow him as his disciples. Many people might know *about* Jesus and the Catholic Faith, but a disciple is someone who knows Jesus personally in the biblical, covenantal sense of being in a close, abiding friendship with him. Jesus isn't only informing us of his teachings; he is proposing a whole new way of living — living like him and living with him at the very center of our lives.

In this stage, we introduce people to the person of Jesus Christ and his saving message of the Gospel (see articles 1.0 – 1.1). We do this primarily through our witness. In the words of Pope St. Paul VI, "Above all, the Gospel must be proclaimed by witness."[1] Our prayer, our example of life, our genuine friendship with the person we are forming all contribute to leading souls closer to Christ. More important than any faith formation program, resource, or study is the living witness of faithful Christians.

The Gospel

But our living witness is not enough. After we have reached out and established a relationship of trust with the people we are leading, we will want to share the Gospel with our words (see article 2.0). According to Paul VI, "There is no true evangelization if the name, the teaching, the life, the promises, the kingdom, and the mystery of Jesus of Nazareth, the Son of God, are not proclaimed."[2] This proclamation can take several forms. However, we have found that a presentation of the Gospel itself and an explicit invitation to say "Yes" to Jesus is one of the most effective.

Acceptance of the Gospel is a crucial moment. Jesus himself says, "This is eternal life, that they know you the only true God, and Jesus Christ whom you have sent" (Jn 17:3). Sometimes we want to teach others all sorts of wonderful truths about the Faith, but when those truths are not preceded by an interior conversion, a true commitment to Christ, they often fail to penetrate deeply the hearts of those who hear them. Therefore, it's crucial that we invite others to surrender to Jesus and allow him to reign over their lives. Once someone personally accepts the Gospel, we can move in our efforts from proclaiming Christ in evangelization (which we call the "Win" phase) to helping them cultivate a "program of life" that deepens one's adherence to Christ (which we call the "Build" phase).[3]

Notes

This is eternal life, that they know you the only true God, and Jesus Christ whom you have sent.

— John 17:3

Build

Once someone has surrendered their life to Christ, it's crucial we "build" them up in the Faith. Within FOCUS, one way we do this is by inviting the person to meet occasionally, either one-on-one or in groups, for ongoing formation in the Faith. This formation aims to give disciples of Jesus an "apprenticeship in the Christian life,"[4] a specific way to begin living out their commitment to Christ. It also allows us to continue journeying with them further along the path of missionary discipleship.

In the words of Paul VI,

> Proclamation only reaches full development when it is listened to, accepted and assimilated, and when it arouses a genuine adherence in the one who has thus received it ... an adherence to the truths which the Lord in his mercy has revealed; still more, an adherence to a program of life — a life henceforth transformed.[5]

That program of life can be summarized in the four key habits of a disciple found at the very beginning of Christianity: prayer, fellowship, the sacramental life, and their formation in Christ's teachings (cf. Acts 2:42) (see articles 3.0 – 3.5). Cultivating these four habits of a disciple helps people deepen their friendship with Christ. Through these practices, disciples begin to think more with the mind of Christ and take on the character of Christ. The goal is for them to become more and more like Jesus.

But we don't just talk about these things. We also model the Christian life for them, accompanying them in living out these basic practices: praying with them, frequenting the sacraments with them, serving the poor with them and, over time, giving them incremental opportunities to practice leading others in these areas themselves.

So, being affectionately desirous of you, we were ready to share with you not only the gospel of God but also our own selves, because you had become very dear to us.

— 1 Thessalonians 2:8

FACT and the High Call to Mission

As we build others up in the practice of the faith, it's important that we also lead them to embrace Christ's mission: "It is unthinkable that a person should accept the Word and give himself to the kingdom without becoming a person who bears witness to it and proclaims it in his turn."[6] The High Call to Mission is an explicit invitation to participate in the Church's mission of evangelization.

While all Christians are called to become missionary disciples, those who are already *faithful* to Christ and the Church, *available* with their time, *contagious* in their Faith, and *teachable* in their heart are ready to answer the call to mission most wholeheartedly and effectively. These four qualities can be summed up with the acronym FACT. Let's look at each one:

- *Faithful* — A missionary disciple must be a faithful disciple first, someone who is fervently living friendship with Jesus Christ, living the four practices of a disciple in Acts 2:42 (prayer, fellowship, the sacraments, and the teaching of the apostles), and *seeking to deepen their intimacy with Christ*. They are also faithful to Jesus in *moral authority*, living beyond reproach, which flows from a willingness to ask more of themselves than they do of others — especially in terms of chastity, sobriety, and excellence (the "Big 3"). And they are *faithful to the Catholic Church* and believe all her teachings.

- *Available* — They must be willing to make time to meet with you and make time to give themselves to the people they are leading. They are willing to make time in their schedule for Christ and the mission to share him with others. Being available doesn't mean they aren't busy. It simply means they are so strongly committed to Christ that they make him and his mission a priority in their lives.

- *Contagious* — They radiate the joy of the Gospel — including the fruits of the spirit (peace, joy, patience, gentleness, etc.) that draw others to Christ (Gal 5:22–23). They also possess the basic human formation necessary to lead and inspire others. This doesn't mean they have to be extroverted, popular, or "cool." Simply, the way they live their life renders the Christian life attractive. They are willing to step out of themselves and draw others in.

- *Teachable* — A missionary disciple is willing to learn from others, including you and other leaders in the ministry, the pastor, and parish staff. They humbly acknowledge they don't have it all figured out and are willing to grow and receive training or correction.

These are four key characteristics we should be looking for in potential leaders — the people to whom we present the High Call to impact the world as a missionary disciple (see articles 4.0 – 4.1).

Once we discern someone is FACT, it's time to share the High Call to Mission (see article 4.2). This is an explicit invitation to participate intentionally in the Church's mission of evangelization. Often, people do not understand the great need for evangelization unless someone explains it to them. The High Call allows you to express clearly both the importance of mission and the role that each of us can play in bringing souls to Christ and forming them to do the same for others.

Send

Once someone has accepted the High Call to Mission, we move into what we call the "Send" phase. A successful missionary disciple isn't someone who merely forms others in the Faith. Indeed, we have not succeeded in forming missionary disciples until the people we serve begin evangelizing and forming missionary disciples of their own who go out and evangelize others. It is only then that the "Little Way of Evangelization" truly begins to take off.

To do this, we need to train Christian disciples in the work of mission. Paul VI writes, "A serious preparation is needed for all workers of evangelization."[7] We've seen already how saints, like St. Ignatius in the story above, did not merely pass on good Christian teaching to their disciples. They also sent them out to find other trustworthy people to train them to do the same for others (2 Tm 2:2) — in other words, St. Ignatius trained his disciples to raise up missionary disciples of their own. The articles in the "Send" section of this book can help you in the work of launching others in the work of missionary discipleship (see articles 5.0 – 6.4).

A Final Note: It's important to note that these stages build upon one another — one stage does not completely end when another begins. We should continue to win hearts to an ever-deeper love for Christ while building them up in the Faith, and we should continue to win and build while sending them on mission. We all need to ponder the Gospel and the call to evangelization repeatedly throughout our lives so we can embrace them more deeply as we grow as missionary disciples.

--- **DISCUSS** ---

Are you prepared to win, build, and send others? Who in your life needs winning, building, and sending? Are you willing to make the sacrifices necessary to help others grow?

PART TWO: THE THREE HABITS OF MISSIONARY DISCIPLES

*Note: This article is divided into two parts: **Win-Build-Send** and **The Three Habits of Missionary Disciples**. It is meant to be broken up into two (or more) conversations.*

THREE HABITS OF MISSIONARY DISCIPLES

If we are going to live this model of Win-Build-Send effectively, we need to be people totally transformed by Christ, people committed to loving him with all our hearts, loving others, and living his mission in the world. Over the years in FOCUS, we have found three key habits of a missionary disciple that seem most important to helping us become the kind of people who can encourage and form other missionary disciples: Divine Intimacy, Authentic Friendship, and Clarity and Conviction about the Little Way of Evangelization.

Divine Intimacy

Like St. Ignatius in the story above, we missionary disciples should have as our first goal to cultivate a deep, personal friendship with Jesus Christ. Evangelization is first and foremost the work of God, and we will be fruitful in the mission of sharing the Gospel only to the extent that we ourselves are abiding in deep union with him. The Gospel tells us, "Apart from me you can do nothing" (Jn 15:5).

How do we grow in our union with Christ? By following the four key practices to which the earliest disciples of Jesus dedicated themselves: prayer, fellowship, the sacraments, and forming our minds with the teachings of Christ (see Acts 2:42). These are the four main ways we continually renew our encounter with Christ and grow in divine intimacy.

Authentic Friendship

In forming missionary disciples, it is not enough to pass on the Gospel message and the teachings of the Church. That is essential, but we must do more. We must genuinely love the people we are serving, accompanying them in life and personally investing ourselves in them through authentic friendship. Think of how Ignatius invested deeply in Francis and Peter: He talked with them, spent with them, gave them his time and attention. We need to do the same with the people we serve. This certainly includes religious activities, but we ought to share every part of their lives except sin.

St. Ignatius lived out the words in 1 Thessalonians 2:8: "So, being affectionately desirous of you, we were ready to share with you not only the gospel of God but also our own selves, because you had become very dear to us."

Personal investment in the people we're serving matters, especially outside of formal settings like Bible study. A true missionary disciple gets to know the people he serves. He doesn't passively wait for people to come to him. He goes out to them, takes an interest in their interests, visits them in their settings, and is a true friend, not simply a small group leader. Consider the words of Pope Francis: "An evangelizing community gets involved by word and deed in people's daily lives ... Evangelizers thus take on the 'smell of the sheep,' and the sheep are willing to hear their voice."[8]

Clarity and Conviction about the Little Way of Evangelization

Think back to the story of St. Ignatius. From the very beginning, he was laboring with clarity and conviction about his mission of evangelization. He invested his life in Francis and Peter. He helped them grow. From the beginning, he sought them out as men whom he would train to evangelize the world.

In 2 Timothy 2:2, Paul exhorts Timothy: "What you have heard from me before many witnesses entrust to faithful men who will be able to teach others also." It isn't enough to teach people the Christian life; we must also teach them to teach others the Christian life. True disciples of Jesus are not only faithful but

Notes

What you have heard from me before many witnesses entrust to faithful men who will be able to teach others also.

— *2 Timothy 2:2*

also fruitful — fruitful in holiness, fruitful in mission.

As we aim to form missionary disciples, we must have both clarity *and* conviction about the Little Way of Evangelization. First, do we have *clarity* about the way Jesus evangelized, about what we have called the "Method Modeled by the Master"? The method Jesus modeled was not one centered on a big way, with a big platform and a big audience. It was a little way. Jesus set out to bring the Gospel to the entire world by investing deeply in twelve men, forming them in the ways of his kingdom and training them to do the same for others. And it was that approach that transformed the world. Second, do we have *conviction* that Jesus' example models for us the *best* way to evangelize? Do we have the *conviction* that if we imitate Jesus' way of evangelization we can be most effective in our mission and help transform our own world today with the Gospel of Jesus Christ? Do we have the *conviction* to prioritize this mission in our lives, making time for this urgent task and pouring our lives out into it? Do we have the *conviction* that this mission is not a job or something extra we do but is at the heart of our identity as disciples of Jesus?

DISCUSS

How can you begin to live these three habits more effectively?

TAKE ACTION

While this article is full of many inspiring, but also challenging, ideas, don't let that overwhelm you. You won't do everything in this article tomorrow. However, it is important that we see the big picture as we begin. Souls are at stake!

One simple first step is to take a look at the "Prayer and Accompaniment Chart" on pg. 159 and the guide following this article. Then, take some time to pray and ask the Lord: Who in your life is he inviting you to invest in as you read about in this article? Write down the names of the people in your life in the appropriate places in the chart. In future articles, you will learn more about praying for these people and accompanying them on the journey of Christian discipleship.

KEY CONCEPTS

Win-Build-Send: A simple way to describe the three general phases that the Church identifies in the process of someone's journey as a Christian disciple, in which they move from conversion to Christ ("Win"), to deepening one's adherence to Christ and the Church ("Build"), to going out to evangelize others ("Send")

FACT — Faithful, Available, Contagious, Teachable: While all Christians are called to become missionary disciples, those who are already faithful to Christ and the Church, available with their time, contagious in their faith, and teachable in their heart are ready to answer the call to mission most wholeheartedly and effectively.

Three Habits of Missionary Disciples: Divine Intimacy, Authentic Friendship, Clarity and Conviction for the Little Way of Evangelization

ADDITIONAL RESOURCES

Making Missionary Disciples by Curtis Martin

SLS18 talk on focusequip.org: *"The Method Modeled by the Master"* by Curtis Martin

Forming Intentional Disciples: The Path to Knowing and Following Jesus by Sherry Weddell

Notes

[1] Paul VI, *Evangelii Nuntiandi*, accessed May 25, 2020, Vatican.va, 21.

[2] Ibid., 22.

[3] Ibid., 23.

[4] Congregation for the Clergy, General Directory for Catechesis, accessed November 5, 2020, Vatican.va, 56.

[5] Paul VI, *Evangelii Nuntiandi*, accessed May 25, 2020, Vatican.va, 23.

[6] Ibid., 24.

[7] Ibid., 73.

[8] Francis, *Evangelii Gaudium*, accessed November 4, 2020, Vatican.va, 24.

SUPPLEMENTAL RESOURCE:

PRAYER AND ACCOMPANIMENT CHART

A GUIDE

The "Prayer and Accompaniment Chart (pg. 159) is a clear and simple tool that you can use as you are investing in others and forming faithful disciples of Jesus who will lead others on mission.

You will see that this tool is divided into the three main categories: Win, Build, and Send. In each category, there is empty space for you to write in the names of people you are serving and even to make notes regarding next steps for you to take as you are accompanying them.

But this tool is not just for planning; it is primarily a tool for prayer. You can use this chart to pray for those you are leading, to entrust them to God and to ask him what he desires to do next in their lives. You can find a printable version of this chart at www.focusequip.org, so you can keep this chart in your Bible, your journal, or wherever else you will have access to it when you pray. This will allow you to keep your mission rooted in prayer and will remind you to be frequently interceding for those the Lord has entrusted to you.

For more on how to lead others along the journey of missionary discipleship, see the article "Walking With Others in Discipleship" on pg. 212.

For more on how to pray for others, see the article "Intercessory Prayer" on pg. 252.

INCARNATIONAL EVANGELIZATION

THE ART OF ACCOMPANIMENT

Optional *Lectio Divina* Prayer

1. Read Matthew 9:10–13.
2. Meditate on the words.
3. Speak to Christ about this passage.
4. Rest and listen in God's presence.
5. Discuss together.

A s a young priest, Fr. Karol Wojtyła lived in troubled times.

His native Poland had been taken over, first by the Nazis and then later by the Soviet-influenced Communists. As his people struggled to live under the Communist regime, laws were put into effect to limit the work of the Church, especially priests. The young people of the time often found themselves lost amid the chaos.

As a good pastor, Fr. Wojtyła went out to his people. He didn't simply schedule talks at a parish and wait for people to come to him; he went out and got involved in their lives. He planned outdoor excursions involving kayaking, camping, hiking, and skiing. He entered the lives of the young people who joined him, getting to know their hopes, dreams, and fears, how they lived their friendships, their struggles in dating relationships, how they made moral choices. He truly shared life with them. They sang. They laughed. They told jokes. They recited poetry.

Fr. Wojtyła was a master of "accompaniment," walking with people amid their daily joys and struggles and witnessing Christ's love to them. He said that God called him "to live with people, everywhere to be with them, in everything but sin."[1] One friend said of him, "We felt that we could discuss anything with him; we could talk about absolutely anything."[2] Others said that he "had mastered the art of listening," that he "was always interested" and that he "always had time."[3] Another simply said, "He lived our problems."[4]

After years of serving as a priest and investing deeply in his friends, Fr. Wojtyła eventually became a bishop, then a cardinal — and then he was elected pope. Many of his friends wondered whether this new responsibility would destroy their friendship. One of them lamented, "We've lost [him]."[5] Only a little while later, however, they found themselves invited to the Vatican. Each year, even with his strenuous schedule as pope, he made time for them in Rome. Just hours before he died, he sent one last message to these same old friends. He loved and cared for these men and women. Being with them wasn't part of his job, a program he was working on, or a task

Everywhere to be with them, in everything but sin.

— *Pope St. John Paul II*

to be completed. He genuinely loved these people and invested his life in them.

The men and women in whom Fr. Wojtyła invested were changed. Some became priests and religious. Others committed themselves to holiness in marriage. All of them lived their Christian lives more faithfully because of his influence. Fr. Wojtyła, now known as Pope St. John Paul II, was a great evangelist — not just as a pope who preached to millions throughout the world, but as a man who went out and invested his life deeply in the people he served in Kraków.

———————————————— **DISCUSS** ————————————————

What stands out to you about the way that Pope St. John Paul II evangelized? How does his example challenge you? How does it encourage you?

INCARNATIONAL EVANGELIZATION

Pope St. John Paull II evangelized by going out, getting involved in people's lives, and sharing his own life with them — a practice that can be called "incarnational evangelization."

Incarnational evangelization is the model of how God evangelized. God didn't stay in heaven waiting for us to find him; he entered our world and sought us out. He came down from heaven, took on human flesh and became like us in all things except sin. He entered our world so that we might one day enter his. This is how God evangelized us.

Jesus also modeled this concept throughout his public ministry. He didn't wait in a synagogue for people to come to him; Jesus went out and built relationships with people by sharing meals with them, conversing with them, praying with them, and hanging out with them. His life revolved around his friendships with people: fishermen, Jewish leaders, tax collectors, prostitutes, and sinners. Jesus calls us to imitate his way of evangelization, to go out to others in the same way he did.

We can also see this principle of incarnational evangelization in the life of St. Paul. During his missionary journeys, while ministering to the people in Thessalonica, Greece, he was willing to give everything of himself so that the people would be able to accept the Gospel. St. Paul sums this up in 1 Thessalonians 2:8: "So, being affectionately desirous of you, we were ready to share with you not only the gospel of God but also our own selves, because you had become very dear to us." He didn't only go around preaching to large audiences and giving talks. He invested himself in people's lives and invited them not only to listen to his message, but also to imitate his way of living — and we are called to do the same.

DISCUSS

What might it look like to "share our very selves," as St. Paul talks about? What do you think the result would be if we just tried to give people the Gospel but not share life with them? Why?

LIVING INCARNATIONAL EVANGELIZATION

How can we begin to live out this model of incarnational evangelization in our lives? Let's discuss a few keys for embracing this important missionary practice.

An Incarnational Heart

One of the first things we need to have to live out incarnational evangelization is what can be called an "incarnational heart" — a heart that yearns, that has a pressing desire, to go out to the peripheries and enter into the lives of those who do not know the Lord. Evangelization can't simply be an obligation. Jesus didn't choose to enter this world because he felt *obliged* to do so or because it was his job, something to check off his list. He was driven by love: love for souls, love for the lost, love especially for those who have no one to love them.

We need to have this same incarnational heart for the lost — a longing to go out to them, to meet them, to share the love of Christ with them. Like Jesus, our desire should be for "all men to be saved and to come to the knowledge of the truth" (1 Tm 2:4). Do our hearts ache for people who don't yet know God in a deep, personal way? Like Christ, true disciples desire to befriend the lost, even in their brokenness.

But how can we develop an incarnational heart if we don't already possess it? Here are two suggestions: First, remember what God has done in your own life — how he changed you, healed you, and saved you. When we watch a great movie or eat at a great restaurant, we often tell people about it. How much more then should we share the greatest blessing in our life, the love of Jesus Christ? Like the first apostles, we should be saying, "we cannot but speak of what we have seen and heard" (Acts 4:20).

Secondly, we need to develop an *eternal perspective* — that is, understanding our life and the lives of others in light of eternity. In the end, every person will either be in heaven with God or lost without him forever. This changes how we think about our daily lives. When we recognize that life is short and that worldly honors, comforts, pleasures, and successes are as nothing compared to knowing Christ Jesus (Phil 3:8), then we are primed to see the work of evangelization as more than

I have become all things to all people so that by all possible means I might save some.

— *1 Corinthians 9:22*

simply a duty or an obligation. It becomes an earnest desire, welling up within us and inspiring us to bring others to Christ, motivating us to reach out to those who do not yet know Christ, even when it's hard or uncomfortable.

Notes

Go Out

Another key to living incarnational evangelization effectively is this: We need to be willing to *go out* and meet people in the midst of their ordinary, daily lives. We need to be willing to hang out where they hang out, to visit their house, to go to their favorite events, to enter their world. As Pope Francis exhorted, "The word of Christ wants to reach all people, in particular those who live in the peripheries of existence. ... We are called to go, to come out from behind our fences and, with zealous hearts, to bring to all the mercy, the tenderness, the friendship of God: this is a job that pertains to everyone."[6] Incarnational evangelization, therefore, requires that we go out to those on the margins, specifically those who are lost and have not yet accepted the Gospel.

The call to go out was Jesus' last command to his apostles. He didn't tell them to wait in Jerusalem for people to come to them, join their programs, attend their meetings, or sign up for their Bible studies. He told them to *go out* to the world: "Go, therefore, and make disciples of all nations" (Mt 28:19). Like the apostles, we shouldn't wait at our homes, the parish, or the campus ministry center and hope people will come to us and seek us out. We must go out to them. We must get involved in their lives, take an interest in their activities, and hang out where they hang out. The Gospel is not a "come to me" Gospel. It is a "go" Gospel. It is a Gospel that is meant to go out.

Sometimes, however, it can be tempting to settle for "Jacuzzi" Christianity. Have you ever sat in a warm Jacuzzi, enjoying time with friends, yet dreading the moment when you have to get out and allow the cold air to whip against your wet skin? Something similar can happen in the Christian life. We can get

so comfortable in our Christian community that we become hesitant to go out to the cold, hurting, and broken world. Instead, God calls us out of our Jacuzzi. He calls us out of our comfortable Catholic bubble to invite others to experience the same joy that we have found in Jesus Christ.

Even the apostles faced this temptation to remain comfortable instead of going out. At the Transfiguration, Peter wanted to build tents and remain on the mountain instead of continuing to Jerusalem where Jesus would suffer. But Jesus leads him back down the mountain. He knows that Peter and the apostles can't simply sit back and remain comfortable. Jesus must continue his mission to the cross and teach his disciples to do the same. Going out, therefore, isn't simply "the FOCUS way" or the way for some; it is *the* way. Every disciple of Jesus is called to go out on mission.

Investing Outside of Formal Settings

Third, after going out to meet people, we need to share life with them and accompany them. On this point, Pope Francis emphasizes, "We need a Church capable of walking at people's sides, of doing more than simply listening to them; a Church which accompanies them on their journey."[7] Evangelization is not simply speaking from a stage, leading a Bible study or faith formation program, or getting together regularly with others for a discipleship meeting. We are called to share our lives with one another: to eat meals together, to hang out on the weekends, to share common interests (including nonreligious ones), and to become part of one another's lives. In sum, we're called to live authentic friendship with the people we serve. It's often when we share life with people outside of formal meetings and faith formation settings that the seeds of faith take deeper root in their souls. All of this helps in sharing the Gospel and inviting people into a deeper encounter with Christ.

Will we invest ourselves personally by giving people not only the Gospel but also our very lives? Will we share life with the people God has entrusted to our care? Will we love them enough to spend time with them outside of Bible study or formal discipleship sessions? Or will we treat them like projects and just schedule meetings?

We should be so willing to get involved in others' lives that we even engage in activities that aren't our preference. If someone loves hiking but we prefer to stay indoors, we'll go hiking. If someone prefers to talk and get coffee, we'll go get coffee. Maybe it's even sacrificing our time and energy. Whatever it might be, we must strive to say with St. Paul, "I have become all things to all men, that I might by all means save some" (1 Cor 9:22).

--------- DISCUSS ---------

How do you need to grow in having an "incarnational heart"? Are you going out or are you living in the Christian Jacuzzi? Are you willing to "become all things to all people" for the sake of Christ and the Gospel?

TAKE ACTION

Incarnational evangelization can look very different depending on the people to whom you are reaching out. Take some time to reflect on the interests of the people in your life. What do they like? Where do they spend their time? What is important to them? How could you enter their lives?

Next, take a minute to write down the names of people in your life. Feel free to use the Prayer and Accompaniment Chart on pg. 159. This resource can help you keep track of the people in your life and discern how you can lead them closer to Christ. Try not to skip anyone, then take a little bit of time to pray about those people God might be asking you to reach out to. Additionally, brainstorm ways that you might be able to share life with these people. Discuss your ideas together and come up with a plan for beginning to live out incarnational evangelization.

KEY CONCEPTS

Incarnational evangelization is the model of how God evangelized. Just as God entered our world, we too must enter other people's lives and meet them where they are to bring them the Gospel.

"Go" Gospel vs. "Come to Me" Gospel: We must go out to share the Gospel. We can't wait for others to come to us. The Gospel is not a "come to me" Gospel. It is a "go" Gospel.[8]

Avoid Jacuzzi Christianity: We must get out of our comfortable Christian community and share God's love with the cold, hurting and broken world.

1 Thessalonians 2:8: "So, being affectionately desirous of you, we were ready to share with you not only the gospel of God but also our own selves, because you had become very dear to us."

ADDITIONAL RESOURCES

Witness to Hope by George Weigel, Ch. 3: "'Call Me Wujek': To Be a Priest"

Evangelii Gaudium, an apostolic exhortation by Pope Francis, Ch. 1: "The Church's Missionary Transformation"

SLS20 talk on focusequip.org: "Authentic Friendship & Incarnational Evangelization" by John Zimmer

Notes

[1] George Weigel, *Witness to Hope* (New York: Harper Perennial, 2005), 104.

[2] Ibid, 105.

[3] Ibid, 102, 105.

[4] Ibid, 107.

[5] Ibid, 256.

[6] Francis, "Homily of His Holiness, Pope Francis, at the Piazza del Plebiscito, Naples (March 21, 2015)," accessed March 30, 2020, Vatican.va.

[7] Francis, "Meeting with the Bishops of Brazil, Address of Pope Francis (July 28, 2013)," accessed March 30, 2020, Vatican.va.

[8] See Francis, *Evangelii Gaudium*, accessed October 2, 2020, Vatican.va, 20.

THE POWER OF YOUR TESTIMONY

Optional *Lectio Divina* Prayer

1. Read 1 Corinthians 2:1–5.
2. Meditate on the words.
3. Speak to Christ about this passage.
4. Rest and listen in God's presence.
5. Discuss together.

Who is one of the most important people in your life: a best friend, a mentor, or a hero?

Take a minute to discuss the influence that person has had on your life.

WHY TESTIMONIES?

Ultimately, what you just did is exactly what you are doing in a testimony. You are simply sharing with others about your truest, best friend, Jesus Christ, and the influence he has had on your life. The Psalmist reflects this experience when he says, "My mouth will tell of your righteous acts, of your deeds of salvation all the day" (Ps 71:55, ESV) and "Come and hear, all you who fear God, and I will tell what he has done for my soul" (Ps 66:16). True Christian disciples want to tell others about Christ. 1 Peter 3:15 says, "Always be prepared to make a defense to anyone who calls you to account for the hope that is in you."

A prepared and practiced testimony is a powerful tool for sharing the Faith. People today tend to be more open to authentic, personal stories of faith than to mere teachings and ideas about the Faith. As Pope St. Paul VI once said, "Modern man listens more willingly to witnesses than to teachers, and if he does listen to teachers, it is because they are witnesses."[1] A personal testimony about the difference Christ has made in your life often touches hearts more than talking about the ideas of the Faith in an abstract way.

Sometimes you might give your testimony in a small group you're leading. Sometimes you might share it with an individual in discipleship. Many times it's good to have your testimony prepared for an opportunity that may come up in conversation when you want to share your faith with someone: a friend when you're out for coffee, someone at work, a relative during a holiday gathering.

Sometimes we might be tempted to think that our story isn't exciting enough. But God has chosen to work in your life in a particular way

for a particular reason. Remember, you are testifying to his work, and that is something to be celebrated. Testimonies about many small ways of turning back to God can be just as powerful as more dramatic stories of conversion.

DISCUSS

What has been your experience with testimonies? Have you ever shared yours before? Why are testimonies a powerful tool for sharing Jesus with the world?

YOUR STORY IN FOUR ACTS

In Scripture, St. Paul uses his testimony to share Christ with others and even proclaim truth to the religious leaders of his day. His story is told at least three times in the book of Acts as a tool for evangelization. Let's look at the way Paul shares his testimony in Acts 26 to help us learn how to share our own testimony. There are four parts, or "acts," in Paul's testimony:

- **1. Life before Jesus Christ**
- **2. Coming to know Jesus Christ**
- **3. Life in Jesus Christ**
- **4. Inviting others to know Jesus Christ**

Act 1: My life before I knew Jesus Christ

Read Acts 26:1–11.

When preparing our testimony, first we need to answer the question, "What kind of a person was I socially, spiritually, and emotionally before I encountered Jesus Christ?"

Within this section, avoid giving too much detail about sins in your past life. Be modest and discreet in what you share. The audience does not need to know details about drunkenness, sexual sin, etc. Simply saying something like, "I was doing things on the weekends I shouldn't have been doing," "I was struggling with purity" or something similar is usually enough to give people a sense of your real struggle without putting a picture in their minds of you in your sin.

────────────── **DISCUSS** ──────────────

What kind of person were you socially, spiritually, or emotionally before you encountered Jesus Christ?

Act 2: How I came to know Jesus Christ

Read Acts 26:12–18.

What happened when you encountered Jesus? Even if the conversion was gradual, the testimony should still have concrete moments or a turning point for the audience to grasp.

If other people were involved in bringing about the conversion, strive to ensure that this section is Christ-centered and not focused on someone else. It is important to remember that Jesus is the main character in your testimony.

Avoid any over-dramatization. God's work in our lives is not always easy to express. Consider how you can organize your story so that people will understand what you have been through and who God is.

———————————————— **DISCUSS** ————————————————

What were some of the key moments in your relationship with Jesus? What did God do to reveal himself to you?

Act 3: My life in Jesus Christ

Read Acts 26:19–23.

What changes have occurred in my life because of my relationship with Jesus? How am I living differently? How has a relationship with Jesus allowed me to live a life that is freer, fuller, and more joyful? Emphasize this part of your testimony because the listener needs to know the significance of a relationship with Jesus. Be attentive to the language you choose here; not everyone listening to your testimony will be familiar with "churchy" language.

Avoid extremes. Try not to come across as a perfected saint. At the same time, don't dwell on the details of your struggles and failures.

———————————————— **DISCUSS** ————————————————

How has a relationship with Jesus allowed you to live a life that is freer, fuller and more joyful? What do you want others to know about having a relationship with Jesus?

Act 4: Inviting the audience to know Christ

Read Acts 26:27–29.

Ask the audience: How will you respond to Jesus Christ, who amazingly offers this salvation to everyone? In a casual setting, you could ask, "Would you like to learn more?" You could even transition from your story to sharing the Gospel directly. Remember, the purpose of a testimony is to lead someone into a deeper relationship with Jesus Christ. Therefore, allow your testimony to be an opportunity for someone to hear the message of the Gospel through your story.

Notes

──────────── **DISCUSS** ────────────

With what message do you want to leave your listener? What step do you want them to take?

──────────────────────────────────────

ELEMENTS OF A GOOD TESTIMONY

As you create and practice the story of Jesus' work in your life, keep these four important elements in mind:

- **CONCRETENESS**: Give the audience details they can relate to. Describe experiences, places, and persons accurately and unambiguously, but don't obsess over details. Include an identifiable and specific turning point (how you came to know Jesus Christ), even if it is just one of many turning points. Your testimony should come across as real and approachable.

- **ACCESSIBILITY**: Describe experiences in such a way that the audience can relate and understand. Choose language free of religious jargon and dense terminology that could separate you from the audience, like "sin," "tabernacle" or "Eucharistic adoration." If you do need to use "churchy" words, take a moment to explain them. Also, ask yourself, "What parts of my story would be especially meaningful to this person?" You will likely emphasize different aspects of your testimony when you are talking to an atheist versus a lukewarm Christian.

Modern man listens more willingly to witnesses than to teachers, and if he does listen to teachers, it is because they are witness.

—*Pope St. Paul VI*

Always be prepared to make a defense to anyone who calls you to account for the hope that is in you.

— 1 Peter 3:15

- **SIMPLICITY**: Include a "plot" or "thread" that is clear and easy to follow, without confusing tangents or elaborate details. Place Jesus Christ at the center of your testimony. He is its hinge. And be sure to keep it short, usually 3–5 minutes or less. Testimonies that are longer than five minutes usually get into too many details and don't have that simple focus for people to follow. A long, meandering testimony loses people and may even turn them off.

DISCUSS

What are some things that might limit the effectiveness of your testimony? How can you eliminate those elements? What would make your testimony powerful?

TAKE ACTION

Based on your discussion of the four "acts" of a testimony, spend some time thinking through and writing down your own testimony. Then, take some time to practice by sharing it with someone whose leadership you trust. Ask them to give you feedback. Practicing frequently will help you develop your story.

Having already prepared and practiced sharing your faith story will help you be ready to share it whenever the opportunity arises. There may be times when you plan to share your testimony, like at your small group or with someone you are leading. Often, though, situations will naturally arise in which you can share about your faith. If someone asks you a question about the Faith, shows curiosity about Christ, asks you why you live the way you do or simply seems like they need encouragement, hope, or inspiration, you want to be prepared to share what Jesus has done in your life.

KEY CONCEPTS

Giving Witness to the Faith: "Modern man listens more willingly to witnesses than to teachers, and if he does listen to teachers, it is because they are witnesses" (Pope St. Paul VI).

1 Peter 3:15: "Always be prepared to make a defense to anyone who calls you to account for the hope that is in you."

The Four Parts of an Effective Testimony, Following St. Paul's Example in Acts 26: 1) Life before Jesus Christ; 2) Coming to know Jesus Christ; 3) Life in Jesus Christ; 4) Inviting others to know Jesus Christ

---

Notes

[1] Paul VI, *Evangelii Nuntiandi*, accessed March 29, 2020, Vatican.va., 41.

5.3

LEADING A TRANSFORMATIVE BIBLE STUDY

Optional *Lectio Divina* Prayer
1. Read Psalm 1:1–6.
2. Meditate on the words.
3. Speak to Christ about this passage.
4. Rest and listen in God's presence.
5. Discuss together.

God's Word is powerful.

When Anthony was about eighteen years old, he lost both of his parents and inherited a considerable amount of wealth. He was walking by a church one day and decided to go in to pray. As he entered, he heard the Gospel for Mass being read: "If you wish to be perfect, go and sell everything you possess and give it to the poor and come, follow me and you will have treasure in heaven" (Mt 19:21). The words from Scripture struck him to the heart: Anthony immediately decided to sell everything he had inherited, give it to the poor, and pursue a life totally dedicated to God. This man who said yes to the Holy Spirit's prompting through God's Word in Scripture went on to become the founder of Desert monasticism, and he is now known as St. Anthony of the Desert.

For the word of God is living and active, sharper than any two-edged sword.

— *Hebrews 4:12*

God's inspired Word in Scripture has the power to change lives. Though not all people will have an encounter with the Bible as dramatic as St. Anthony did that day, every ordinary Christian should be challenged, encouraged, and guided by the sacred words of Scripture in their daily lives. In these sacred books, we encounter not merely the words of men from a long time ago, but the words of God, speaking to us today through those human words.

This is one reason why small-group Bible studies can make a significant impact on people's lives. We gather to read not any ordinary book, but rather the inspired Word of God, speaking to us today. As Scripture itself attests, "For the word of God is living and active, sharper than any two-edged sword, piercing to the division of soul and spirit, of joints and marrow, and discerning the thoughts and intentions of the heart" (Heb 4:12). As they did for St. Anthony, the Scriptures have an incredible ability to open hearts and impact those who read them, even today.

But that's not all. Participants in a Bible study not only encounter God in his Word, but they also encounter God in their fellowship with each other as they consider how God's Word can be applied to

their lives today. Hearing how others are applying Scripture to their lives can be very encouraging, reminding us that we're not alone in our faith journey; there are others striving to live the Christian life as well. Hearing about their struggles, trials, joys, and triumphs in applying God's Word to their lives can inspire us to go deeper in our faith.

——————————— **DISCUSS** ———————————

Have you experienced the power of Scripture in your own life? Why is it significant that Scripture still has the power to transform us today, thousands of years after it was written?

GOALS FOR BIBLE STUDY

> *Ignorance of Scripture is ignorance of Christ.*
>
> — St. Jerome

Lots of things can be accomplished within a Bible study. That's why, as you begin to lead one, you need to know your goals. What exactly are you trying to accomplish? We encourage you to focus on these three goals: divine intimacy, authentic friendship, and clarity and conviction for the Little Way of Evangelization.

- **Divine Intimacy:** The purpose of a Bible study is not simply to learn information or be part of a club, but to facilitate a deeper encounter with God that changes people's lives.

192

Notes

- **Authentic Friendship:** Your participants can learn about God's Word by themselves. The power of a small group is the experience of learning from one another. The friendships formed within a Bible study are crucial for transformation and accountability, and the insights shared between participants can uncover even deeper understanding.

- **The Little Way of Evangelization:** Bible studies also provide a setting to guide others to become missionary disciples themselves. As good as it is to form friendships and grow closer to God, don't let your study stop there; be on the lookout for others whom God may be calling you to form as missionary disciples who will go on to evangelize and lead other small groups of their own.

Keep in mind, you don't have to be a Scripture scholar or have an electric personality to be an effective Bible study leader. Anyone who is following Jesus in divine intimacy, who is willing to build authentic friendships, and who is committed to Christ's method of winning, building, and sending can be effective.

–––––––––––––––––––– **DISCUSS** ––––––––––––––––––––

What has been your experience of small groups or Bible studies? Did your group live out any of these habits well? In what ways? As you prepare to lead a study, how can you keep these three goals in mind?

THREE ASPECTS OF LEADING A GREAT STUDY

Now that you know why you should lead a study and what your primary goals are, let's turn to the other three aspects of leading a great Bible study: preparation, skills, and personal investment.

PREPARATION

You won't be able to lead a good discussion if you haven't taken the time to properly prepare for your study. Here are some tips for preparing well:

- **Pick Out the Right Study:** Choose a study that meets the needs of your group. FOCUS resources can be found at focusequip.org. For those new to Bible study, we recommend starting with "The Crux" and "The Story of Salvation."

- **Pray and Share from Your Own Encounter with God's Word:** Just reading the materials and Leader's Guide ahead of time is not enough. Prayerfully ponder how the biblical passages challenge you or encourage you personally. Your Bible study will be more authentic the more you share from your own encounter with God's word. Remember, this is God's work; leading a Bible study is an invitation to rely on the Holy Spirit, not simply your own ability.

- **Prepare Questions for Encounter:** Look at the discussion questions and select questions that will be meaningful for your group. Adjust or rephrase questions, if necessary. Ask yourself, "What questions will have the greatest impact on my group?"

- **Select a Few Main Truths to Emphasize:** As you read through the study you are about to lead, determine one to three key truths you want to share with your group. Keep your focus on those points. Whatever else happens in the study, make sure you focus on these key truths and don't get lost in too many details, side conversations, or tangents. Always bring things back to the big ideas you want everyone to come away with.

─────────────── **DISCUSS** ───────────────

What would it look like for you to prepare well each week for Bible study? Are you willing to make the sacrifices necessary — particularly with your time — to prepare well?

SKILLS

Various skills are also necessary for leading transformative Bible studies. Let's look at a few key skills that will allow you to lead well.

- **Hospitality:** Making sure everyone feels comfortable and welcome will make a huge difference for your Bible study, especially in the beginning before everyone knows each other. Here are some tips for great hospitality:

  - Find an accessible and informal location that can be used or reserved each week. Ask yourself, "What is the easiest location for my group to access? Where will they feel most comfortable?"

  - Provide food and refreshments, especially during the first few weeks. People love food! It also gives the participants something natural to do as they begin to arrive and chat with one another. As your group grows, consider getting others more involved by rotating this responsibility. The more others are engaged, the better.

  - Consider using your first night of study just to get to know one another, begin to form friendships and briefly preview what you'll be studying. Make this night fun and lighthearted, since this will encourage your members to come back!

  - Build up relationships in your study. Ask good questions that allow your members to share their lives. Use your

knowledge of various members to connect them with one another and to uncover common interests.

- Finally, find a length of time for your study that works and stick to it. Some Bible study members will fall off if you aren't consistent. Begin and end on time. Even if you have to start late, respect your group's time by ending on time.

Facilitating an Encounter, Not Teaching: As the leader of a Bible study, you aren't primarily a teacher, lecturing or explaining everything about the study each week. You should not be doing all the talking. Remember, the goal is to allow your participants to encounter God's Word in the Scriptures and in each other. What can you do to facilitate conversation well? Here are some tips:

- Use great questions to draw out the conversation. How can you use questions that lead the group to reflect on their own experiences and on what the Scriptures are revealing?

- Allow other members of the group to answer questions. Just because someone asks a question doesn't mean you need to be the one to answer it. Present the question to the entire group, and allow several people to contribute to an answer. Afterward, you can clarify, if necessary.

Generating an Engaging Conversation — Three Roles: Within your study, you have three key roles for developing a great discussion: the trail guide, the traffic cop, and the cheerleader:

- **Trail Guide:** If you've ever gone hiking, you know how helpful it can be to have a guide who has been on the trail before. They know which way to go, when to stop, and where all the good views are. With your Bible study, you need to be a trail guide — someone who has been through the material before and who knows where to go to make the discussion great.

- **Traffic Cop:** Have you ever watched a traffic cop in action? Their ability is almost an art form as they smoothly direct people and cars with just the power of their hands and a whistle. Numerous obstacles and traffic jams can prevent your study from flowing properly. Like a traffic cop, you may need to stop certain discussions or tangents. At the same time, you may need to encourage shy members of the group to speak up and share. Be mindful of the conversation to make sure everyone is participating and direct the discussion toward topics that will build up your group.

- **Cheerleader:** Even when their team is struggling, a great cheerleader watches the games, cheers loudly, and wears their team's gear. As the leader of a Bible study, you need to cheer on your study. Smile, encourage participation and create an environment where people know you are supportive of them and interested in what they have to say. Give some positive affirmation when someone contributes, even if their comments are not perfectly on point. When people know they are cared about and appreciated, they are more likely to engage in the discussion.

You can know you are facilitating a study well when your study looks like a good volleyball game: The conversation should go back and forth "over the net," involving a variety of participants. As the leader, you serve the ball by asking a good question. Then someone answers, setting the ball up for someone else in the group to comment, who then passes it along to another. When the volley is over, you serve up another question.

Also, if you struggle with facilitating a dynamic Bible study, don't be afraid to learn from someone else. Go to another leader's study and observe what makes their study successful.

――――――――――――――――― **DISCUSS** ―――――――――――――――

What skills do you need to grow in as a Bible study leader? How can you grow in these skills? Where might you need help from someone else?

PERSONAL INVESTMENT

For full transformation and conversion of heart, relational investment inside and outside of Bible study is crucial. You are forming people, not simply conducting a regular meeting. Here are some tips for great investment in your Bible study members:

- Spend some time with them outside of study. Jesus didn't spend time with his disciples only once a week in a class or during moments of formal teaching; he shared life with them through his interest in them and the time he spent with them during everyday moments of life.

- Make invitations to other events and activities. How else can you spend time with your participants? What other activities will help them grow?

- Witness a life well-lived. Ask yourself, "Am I reinforcing the truths I am teaching in Bible study by the way I live?" As leaders, our lives should reflect what we are teaching. If we don't witness to the truths we are teaching, the members of our Bible study likely won't accept what is being taught. We need to live the truths we are teaching.

DISCUSS

How can you make a deeper investment in the members (or potential members) of your Bible study?

TAKE ACTION

Now it's time to begin your Bible study. Here are some tips for getting started:

- First, pray that the Lord leads you to the people he wants for your study.

- Brainstorm potential members of your Bible study, being careful not to limit yourself. Whom does God want you to invite?

- Pray that God would open the hearts of these people to attend the study.

- Make time to invite each person personally. When Jesus invited the disciples to follow him, he didn't post a scroll in the town square or leave messages at their houses. Instead, he approached each one individually and invited them personally.

- Follow up with everyone and make sure they have all the details for the first study.

- Take time to prayerfully prepare your study material or the activities you will use to get to know one another. Intercede for the members of your group.

- Send reminders to everyone on the day of your study or the day before. People forget sometimes. Don't let that get in the way of a great study.

Encourage one another and build one another up, just as you are doing.

— 1 Thessalonians 5:11

- Especially for the first study, take extra time to allow the group to get to know each other. Forming these bonds is a critical component for keeping people interested.

- Finally, be persistent. A great study may require several invitations or an additional investment of time and energy. Put in the extra work to make your study great. Keep praying, keep making invitations, and keep working on your Bible study skills.

DISCUSS

Do you have any fears about leading a Bible study? What would help you overcome those fears? What steps do you need to take to develop a great Bible study?

KEY CONCEPTS

Inspiration of Scripture: The Bible is inspired by God. When we read Scripture, we encounter God's Word speaking to us today, his divine Word communicating through the human words of the sacred writers.

God's Word is powerful: "For the word of God is living and active, sharper than any two-edged sword, piercing to the division of soul and spirit, of joints and marrow, and discerning the thoughts and intentions of the heart" (Heb 4:12).

The three goals of a Bible study: Divine Intimacy, Authentic Friendship and the Little Way of Evangelization

The three roles to play while leading: Trail Guide, Traffic Cop, and Cheerleader

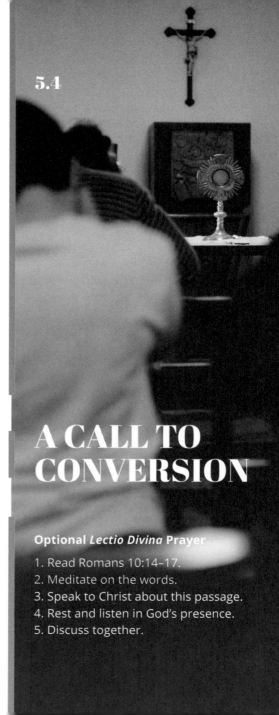

SHARING THE GOSPEL

A CALL TO CONVERSION

Optional *Lectio Divina* Prayer

1. Read Romans 10:14–17.
2. Meditate on the words.
3. Speak to Christ about this passage.
4. Rest and listen in God's presence.
5. Discuss together.

When starting his religious order, the Jesuits, St. Ignatius of Loyola planned to invite his dear friend Francis Xavier to serve as a scholar and teacher for their growing movement.

But his plans were soon interrupted. King John of Portugal requested that the Jesuits send missionaries to his recently acquired territory in India. Ignatius appointed two of his Jesuits for the task, but when one became seriously ill, he was forced to send someone else. With great hesitation, Ignatius sent Francis Xavier, knowing that he would probably never see his dear friend ever again.

After his departure, Francis Xavier would send letters back to Ignatius to update him on his mission. Francis Xavier described how he invited thousands of people to accept the Gospel and be baptized. He saw hundreds of thousands of conversions, but he was still frustrated that more couldn't be done. He wrote to Ignatius,

> Many, many people fail to become Christians, simply for the lack of a teacher of the Christian faith! Often I think of running throughout the universities of Europe, and principally Paris and the Sorbonne, there to shout at the top of my voice, like one who had lost his senses—to tell those men whose learning is greater than their wish to put their knowledge to good use, how many souls, through their negligence, must lose Heaven and end up in hell.[1]

While not all of us are called to go to India to evangelize, Francis Xavier's conviction holds true wherever we are. There are people all around us who aren't living in friendship with Jesus Christ and his Church for one main reason: There is no one willing to help them! As St. Paul says in his letter to the Romans, "how are they to believe in him of whom they have never heard? And how are they to hear without a preacher?" (Rom 10:14).

As Catholics, each one of us is called to preach the Gospel in two ways: witness and words. As Pope St. Paul VI reminds us, "Modern

man listens more willingly to witnesses than to teachers, and if he does listen to teachers, it is because they are witnesses."[2] Our witness is essential. Still, "even the finest witness will prove ineffective in the long run if it is not explained."[3] St. Francis of Assisi is often quoted as saying, "Preach the Gospel at all times, and, if necessary, use words." We have no evidence that St. Francis ever said this; instead, the Church, saints, and Scripture all testify that we must proclaim the Gospel in words also (1 Cor 9:16). Indeed, "there is no true evangelization if the name, the teaching, the life, the promises, the kingdom, and the mystery of Jesus of Nazareth, the Son of God, are not proclaimed."[4] We can't just hope that those around us will somehow stumble upon the Christian faith on their own. Like St. Francis Xavier, we must proclaim the Gospel to them directly — *with words*.

DISCUSS

Has someone shared the Gospel with you? What was that experience like? Are you convinced of the need to share the Gospel?

PROCLAIMING THE GOSPEL: THE MESSAGE

The Gospel is the "good news" of Christ's life, death, and resurrection for the sake of our salvation. This message is sometimes called the *kerygma*, which itself means "proclamation." It is the essential message of salvation through Jesus Christ.[5]

Though there are numerous ways to summarize the Gospel — and though there have been entire books written on examining its depths — it is important that we share the Gospel with others in a way that is simple, compelling, and easy to understand.

You may have previously discussed the Gospel discipleship article, or perhaps someone invited you to welcome Jesus as the Lord of your life through a conversation or using Scripture. In whatever way you have heard it, the Gospel message generally consists of a few points that contain the basic message of our salvation. While there are many ways to express the saving message of Jesus Christ, the points in this article on the Gospel are based on an image from St. Catherine of Siena in her *Dialogue*, in which she describes Christ as a bridge between God and sinful humanity.[6] These points are developed more in depth on pg. 42. But here is a brief summary:

- **Relationship: What We're Made For** — We are made for a relationship with God.

- **Rebellion: The Chasm** — Our relationship with God was broken by sin. An infinite chasm separated us from God. We have a desire for a lasting happiness that only comes from a relationship with God, but we are unable to amend our relationship with him by ourselves. We are finite, and only an infinite love can bridge the infinite gap caused by sin.

- **Reconciliation: The God-Man Solution** — As fully human, Jesus can represent us and offer an act of love on behalf of the entire human family. But because he is also fully divine, Jesus' act of love far surpasses anything a mere human could ever offer. It is an infinite gift of love that he offered for us to the Father on the cross. Jesus, therefore, is the bridge between sinful humanity and the all-holy God.

- **Re-Creation: Transformation in Christ** — Jesus has not only died to offer us forgiveness; he has also risen to fill us with his life so that we can be transformed in him. He wants to make us a "new creation"[7] (2 Cor 5:17). This process of sanctification happens in and through the Church. All that Jesus won for us in his death and resurrection comes to us through the Church — through its teachings, its sacraments, and the fellowship of believers in the communion of saints.

- **Response: "Follow Me"** — Jesus invites each of us to respond to the Gospel and follow him as his disciples.

For a deeper exposition of these points, please be sure to read and pray through the Gospel article on pg. 40, which explains each of these points in greater depth. A deep foundational understanding of the Gospel message is critical to share it well!

As you grow in understanding of the Gospel message, you can also turn to various Scripture verses that help express the kerygma. The *Directory for Catechesis*, for example, identifies several Scripture verses that express the saving message of Jesus Christ. Here are a few of its recommended verses:[8]

- Mark 1:15: "The kingdom of God is at hand; repent, and believe in the gospel."

- John 3:16: "For God so loved the world that he gave his only Son, that whoever believes in him should not perish but have eternal life."

- John 10:10: "I came that they may have life, and have it abundantly."

Pope Francis also once summarized the Gospel this way: "Jesus Christ loves you; he gave his life to save you; and now he is living at your side every day to enlighten, strengthen, and free you."[9]

These passages proclaim to us in simple form the message of salvation in Jesus Christ. It is this basic Christian message that we should ponder over and over again throughout our lives and share with others, often and explicitly.

Notes

───────────────── **DISCUSS** ─────────────────

What is the Gospel? How would you summarize it? How have you heard this message powerfully shared?

MAKING THE INVITATION

We should always be ready share the Gospel — in a conversation with a friend, with our family at home, or even to a stranger who needs to hear the hope of Christ. Often, however, we want to share the Gospel with specific people: those in our small groups and our faith formation programs, for example, or those we are mentoring in the Faith. In these situations, it's probably best to share the Gospel at a specific time and place, letting the other person know that you'd like to talk to them about the Faith.

You'll want to **prepare** ahead of time how you'll present the Gospel message to them and how you'll make the invitation for them to make Jesus the center of their life. We'd encourage you to use the Gospel discipleship article (see pg. 40), which lays out each of the points of the Gospel message in a conversational but powerful way. You may also decide to build your presentation around some passages of Scripture or incorporate your testimony.

Once you decide how you will share the Gospel, it's important that you **practice** a few times so that you feel confident sharing the message clearly and boldly. It even helps to practice with someone and have them give you feedback. The more you practice sharing the Gospel, the more confident you will be making this powerful invitation.

Many, many people fail to become Christians, simply for the lack of a teacher of the Christian faith.

— *St. Francis Xavier*

When you sit down with someone to share the Gospel, you can start the conversation casually. Take some time to catch up and thank them for taking some time with you. After that, it's time to **share** the message you prepared. Try to make this conversational as well, such as asking the other person questions to give them an opportunity to enter the conversation and share their thoughts.

Finally, don't forget the most powerful part of sharing the Gospel: **Invite** the other person to say "Yes" to Jesus as Lord of their entire life. If they say yes, take some time to pray together and invite them to take a step in their faith — by coming to Mass, joining a Bible study, praying daily, or going to confession. If they say no or are uncertain, thank them for having the conversation with you and ask them what questions they still have or if there is anything they want to learn more about. This is a great chance for you to continue to walk with them and introduce them to Jesus and the Faith in new ways.

———————————————— **DISCUSS** ————————————————

How do you think the people in your life would best receive the message of the Gospel? How could you prepare for these conversations?

OVERCOMING OBSTACLES

At this point in the article, you might be really excited, but you also might be a little uncertain. You might be thinking, *Am I ready for this? Is this really what I'm supposed to be doing? Is this Catholic?* Let's address some common objections to sharing the Gospel:

- *Is this Catholic?* Some might wonder if forming others in catechesis and leading them to the sacraments is more important than sharing the Gospel. But many practicing Catholics have not yet been evangelized. They may be going through the motions, even believing the right things, but they have not truly encountered Christ and surrendered their lives to him. They do not have a "living sense of the faith"[10] — or, in the words of Pope Francis, they "lack a meaningful relationship to the Church and no longer experience the consolation born of faith."[11] While saying yes to Christ isn't the only step in one's faith life, it is the most foundational.

Presenting the Gospel seems forced or impersonal. Let's be honest: Sharing the Faith can be awkward sometimes. But so can asking someone out on a first date or interviewing for an important job. Sometimes great things require us to step out of our comfort zones. By building strong relationships and sharing the Gospel honestly from the heart, you can make it more natural. But don't let a little awkwardness prevent someone from knowing Jesus.

I don't know if I'm ready; I don't feel equipped. That may be so. But God doesn't call the equipped; he equips the called. The real question is, are you willing? Do you want someone to come to know Jesus? Then pray, practice with a good friend or mentor (maybe even multiple times), and share. Imagine what could happen if they say yes!

DISCUSS

Do you have any hesitations about sharing the Gospel? How can you overcome these?

For I am not ashamed of the gospel: it is the power of God for salvation to every one who has faith.

— Romans 1:16

TAKE ACTION

It's time to start practicing how to share the Gospel. Take some time to read the Gospel article on pg. 40, and then practice sharing the points of the Gospel in an engaging and authentic way with another faithful person. Ask them to give you feedback on how you can improve. Adjust your presentation if something doesn't go over well or doesn't feel natural. Once you have your presentation prepared, you will be ready to share the Gospel more effectively whenever you need to, whether it be in the context of a small group study or discipleship or a conversation with a friend.

KEY CONCEPTS

The Message of the Gospel: Based on St. Catherine of Siena's image of the bridge, the Gospel can be summarized in these simple steps:

- Relationship: What We're Made For
- Rebellion: The Chasm
- Reconciliation: The God-Man Solution
- Re-Creation: Transformation in Christ
- Response: "Follow Me"

ADDITIONAL RESOURCES:

Directory for Catechesis, in particular paragraphs 57 – 60.

Notes

[1] Milton Walsh. *Witness of the Saints: Patristic Readings in the Liturgy of the Hours* (Ignatius Press: San Francisco, 2012), 638.

[2] Paul VI, *Evangelii Nuntiandi*, accessed September 3, 2020, Vatican.va, 41.

[3] Ibid, 22.

[4] Ibid.

[5] See also: Pontifical Council for the Promotion of the New Evangelization. *Directory for Catechesis* (USCCB: Washington, 2020), 57 – 60.

[6] See *St. Catherine of Siena: The Dialogue*.

[7] Pontifical Council for Culture, "Concluding Document of the Plenary Assembly: The *Via Pulcritudinous*, Priviliged Pathway for Evangelization and Dialogue (2006), accessed November 17, 2020, Vatican.va, III.1.

[8] See also *Directory for Catechesis* par. 58, footnote 5.

[9] Francis, *Evangelii Gaudium*, accessed September 3, 2020, Vatican.va, 164.

[10] John Paul II, *Redemptoris Missio*, accessed September 7, 2020, Vatican.va, 33.

[11] Francis, *Evangelii Gaudium*, accessed October 2, 2020, Vatican.va, 14.

5.5

WALKING WITH OTHERS IN DISCIPLESHIP

Optional *Lectio Divina* Prayer

1. Read 2 Timothy 2:1–5.
2. Meditate on the words.
3. Speak to Christ about this passage.
4. Rest and listen in God's presence.
5. Discuss together.

What do you think of when you picture St. Paul?

Many Christians remember the pre-conversion Paul, who "persecuted the Church of God violently and tried to destroy it" (Gal 1:13). He is well known for his dramatic conversion to Christianity on the road to Damascus, his missionary work as the great apostle to the Gentiles, and his writings, which make up a major portion of the New Testament.

But Scripture shows us another side of Paul, a side not as well-known but just as influential for the Church and the world: his intentional discipleship with those he was forming in the Faith.

Paul's traveling companion for much of his missionary journey was a young Christian named Timothy. Upon arriving in Lystra on his second missionary journey, Paul learned of the sound reputation of this faithful young Christian. By the end of Paul's visit there, Timothy was inspired to leave everything behind and to join the great apostle on mission.[1]

As Paul and Timothy journeyed together, Paul intentionally trained Timothy to lead. Paul sent Timothy first to Thessalonica and later to Macedonia to encourage the Christians there, exhorting him to "[l]et no one despise your youth, but set the believers an example in speech and conduct, in love, in faith, in purity" (1 Tm 4:12). After each assignment, Timothy returned to his mentor for even more training in mission.

After a period of deep investment and laboring together, Paul trusted that he had formed Timothy well enough to let him lead on his own — so he sent Timothy on an extended mission to a troubled community in Ephesus. As Timothy fought to address false teachings there, Paul encouraged him: "I hope to come to you soon, but I am writing these instructions to you so that, if I am delayed, you may know how one ought to behave in the household of God" (1 Tm 3:14).

A few years later, knowing his own death was near, Paul summoned Timothy to Rome.[2] In his last letter, Paul writes with gratitude for their friendship: "I remember you constantly in my prayers. As I remember your tears, I long day and night to see you, that I might be filled with joy" (2 Tm 1:3–4). But Paul also makes it clear: Timothy's charge was to take up the torch that had been handed on to him by Paul over their many years together and to continue to spread Christ's teachings to the ends of the earth (cf. 2 Tm 2:2). Their "partnership in the Gospel" bore great fruit through their own ministries, but the ripple effects were only beginning (Phil 1:5).

DISCUSS

What do you find most inspiring or surprising about this story of the early Church? What strikes you about Paul's investment in Timothy? What does it reveal to you about discipleship that Paul and Timothy were on mission for more than 15 years together, even when their lives took them apart from one another?

THE IMPORTANCE OF DISCIPLESHIP

St. Paul was an incredible missionary in many ways. But there was only one St. Paul. He couldn't be everywhere at once, and his days on earth were numbered. His missionary efforts produced great fruit in his time, but his investment in passing on the Faith and raising leaders who could continue that mission after he was gone was what truly produced a lasting impact.

The goal of every missionary disciple is to help form other missionary disciples who will live out the Little Way of Evangelization wherever the Lord calls them. It is inviting them to a journey of imitation, an invitation to "be imitators of me, as I am of Christ" (1 Cor 11:1), as Paul himself invited the early Christians to do.

To fulfill this mission, we are called to accompany others in discipleship like St. Paul did, which involves so much more than just teaching ideas about the Faith. It entails walking with them through the ups and downs of both their spiritual journey and all other parts of life. It is not about a club or a program but a commitment to a person, to their spiritual growth and to the mission the Lord has in store for them. We can do that by doing for others what Paul did for Timothy.

> *Be imitators of me, as I am of Christ.*
>
> — *1 Corinthians 11:1*

--------- **DISCUSS** ---------

How has someone led you like Paul did for Timothy? When considering what they did, what was most transformative for your own understanding of mission?

LEADING LIKE ST. PAUL

How do you begin investing in others the way Paul invested in Timothy? How do you prepare them to be built up in relationship with Christ and sent on mission? We can follow St. Paul's example of forming missionary disciples in four ways:

- *Paul shared life with the people he served.*

- *Paul gave Timothy intentional training for ministry.*

- *Paul invited Timothy to go out on mission together with him.*

- *Paul sent Timothy to entrust the mission to others.*

Let's look more closely at each of these elements of walking with another in discipleship.

Sharing Life with the People We Serve

Paul didn't just lead Timothy in a Bible study or have one-on-one training meetings with him. Paul spent a lot of time with Timothy outside of formal meetings. As they journeyed together on mission, Paul and Timothy shared much of everyday life together: meals, prayer, service and many long days of travel. Paul loved Timothy as a close friend, sharing with him not only the Gospel but his very life (cf. 1 Thes 2:8). Paul cared not only for Timothy's mission. He cared about Timothy.

You are called to do the same as you walk with those in your life. You have probably been doing this already; continue to share life with the people you are leading by cooking meals together, visiting the Blessed Sacrament together, and pursuing other ways to share life together.

Intentional Training for Mission

Paul took the time to teach Timothy how to lead and form others during their time together; when they were apart, Paul wrote letters to Timothy instructing him what to teach, advising him on how to deal with conflict, and encouraging him in keeping his own faith. Paul formed Timothy both in his own personal growth and in practical training for mission.

Once someone in your life has made a commitment to Christ and desires to grow in their faith, they are ready to be intentionally formed. This intentional formation looks different depending on where the person in whom you are investing is in their journey.

- When the person you are investing in is in the "Build" phase, you will likely want to meet occasionally to talk about their walk with Christ, particularly in the basic Christian practices of Acts 2:42: prayer, fellowship, the sacraments, and the teaching of the apostles (see articles 3.0 – 3.5). But we don't just want to *talk about* these ideas. We also want to create opportunities for the person to have *experiences* together in prayer, sacraments, Christian fellowship, and faith formation.

- Once someone has accepted the High Call to Mission, it is best to meet regularly (with a group of other missionary disciples, if possible) for intentional formation and training for mission. This is where you will discuss the "Send" articles (see articles 5.0 – 6.4), practice your mission skills, and spend intentional time going on mission together.

Going on Mission Together

Paul did not simply give Timothy lessons on what to do in the mission field: He modeled mission for him and gave him opportunities to practice. Timothy learned from Paul as he watched him preach the Gospel, answer questions, debate unbelievers, call sinners to repent,

and encounter rejection, scorn, and even imprisonment. Paul did not just *teach* Timothy about mission; he also *lived it alongside him*.

In your own discipleship, it is important to go on mission together, embodying how Jesus sent his disciples out two by two throughout the Gospels (cf. Lk 10:1). For example, attend the Bible study of the person you are leading and discuss with them afterward what went well and where they could improve. Invest in new people together. Go together to a parish event and meet new people. These are just a few of the ways you can go on mission together.

Seeing Beyond Timothy

In their missionary efforts, Paul was not only concerned about Timothy but also about those Timothy was leading. In one of his letters, Paul instructs Timothy: "What you have heard from me before many witnesses entrust to faithful men who will be able to teach others also" (2 Tm 2:2). Paul was frequently "seeing beyond Timothy" to those Timothy was investing in, and to those being reached beyond them. As you walk with others, your conversations and investment in others should not just be focused on the two of you but also on the mission entrusted to you and how you are entrusting it to others.

DISCUSS

What are some practical ways you can share life with the people in whom you are investing? What intentional formation do you think Jesus wants them to receive next? What could you learn by going out on mission with someone else alongside you? How will you ensure that your discipleship relationship is not just focused inward on the two of you but remains looking outward at those in whom you are investing?

PITFALLS TO INTENTIONAL DISCIPLESHIP

While this article (and previous ones) have given you a vision for how best to lead others in discipleship, you might still need to practice, to make mistakes, and to learn from them. As you are learning to walk with others in discipleship, here are three pitfalls to avoid:

- **Buddy:** Be careful not to let your time together slip into just being "buddies" while letting intentional formation fall to the wayside. Your conversations might begin with what's going on in your lives, but your conversations should center around mission and your next steps in evangelization.

- **Counselor:** Your role for those you are accompanying is not to be a counselor or a spiritual director. If the person you are walking with does need more substantial spiritual, mental, or emotional guidance, help them seek out a priest, a good counselor, a spiritual director, or other helpful resources!

- **Boss:** Be aware not to let your discipleship relationship be reduced to nothing more than a weekly meeting or discussions solely about goals, progress, and accountability. Falling into the "boss" mentality leaves out the one who's really in charge of mission: Jesus himself! Your role is more like a mentor, one

What you have heard from me before many witnesses entrust to faithful men who will be able to teach others also.

— *2 Timothy 2:2*

who encourages, listens, guides, coaches, and helps someone else progress in their mission and toward heaven.

—————————— DISCUSS ——————————

Which of these three pitfalls do you imagine yourself falling into more easily? What kind of accountability will you need to keep your discipleship intentional and authentic?

TAKE ACTION

Now that you know the elements of intentional discipleship, it's time to start preparing and living it out. As you plan and prepare to invest in others, follow these four steps:

- *Pray:* Take time each week to pray for the people in whom you are investing. Let Jesus guide you to the next conversation you need to have or the next skill the person in whom you are investing is ready to learn and practice.

- *Prepare:* Based on your prayer, decide what you would like to teach, discuss, or do in your next intentional meeting time. If you decide to discuss a Discipleship Article, take time to read and prepare the article (see Introduction article). If you are practicing some mission skill, take time to think through how you will coach the person or group(s) you're leading and offer feedback.

- *Teach and Learn:* During your meeting, use what you prepared to create an authentic conversation and mission experience. Ask good questions and feel free to depart from what you had planned, if the Holy Spirit leads. One way to structure your time together looks like this:

- 5 – 10 mins: Open in prayer (*Lectio Divina*, intercessory prayer, spontaneous prayer, etc.)

- 30 – 40 mins: Intentional formation or mission practice (discussing a Discipleship Article, reading or listening to a supplemental resource from an article, going out and practicing a mission skill, problem-solving to overcome an obstacle in mission, etc.)

- 10 – 15 mins: Debrief and discuss next steps

Please note: This is not a required structure, but rather a guide to help you ensure that you are incorporating the various pieces of discipleship in your time together. Feel free to adapt this as necessary.

Next Steps: At the end of your meeting, discuss any takeaways and decide what next steps you both need to take to practice and grow in mission. This is where the vision and the ideas from your conversation become a lived habit that can transform your life.

Using these four steps, plan 2–3 weeks of formation and investment for someone in whom you are investing. Consider: How will you intentionally form them to help them grow in their walk of faith? In what ways will you share life with them, in addition to the times of formation? How will you pursue the habits of Acts 2:42 together?

KEY CONCEPTS

Seeing Beyond Timothy: We must ensure that the people we are leading will faithfully entrust the vision and mission of evangelization to those whom they are leading, according to 2 Tm 2:2: "What you have heard from me before many witnesses entrust to faithful men who will be able to teach others also."

Notes

Notes

[1] Scott Hahn, "Timothy," *Catholic Bible Dictionary* (New York: Doubleday, 2009), 914.

[2] *Ignatius Catholic Study Bible: New Testament, Revised Standard Version (2nd ed.)*, comp. Curtis Mitch, ed. Scott Hahn (San Francisco: Ignatius Press, 2001), 395.

PERSONAL
FORMATION

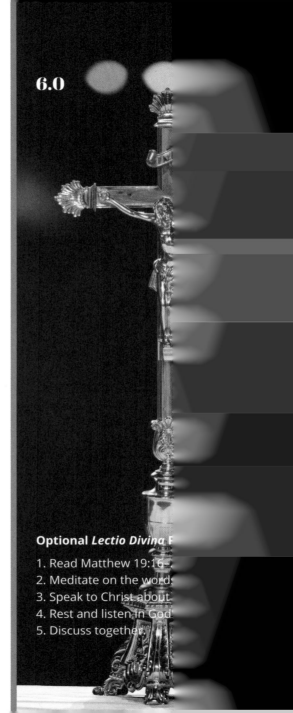

6.0

PURSUING CHRIST-LIKE CHARACTER

Optional *Lectio Divina*

1. Read Matthew 19:16–
2. Meditate on the word
3. Speak to Christ about
4. Rest and listen in God'
5. Discuss together.

"What do I still lack?"

That was the amazing question a young person once asked Jesus some 2,000 years ago. The young man had already been a very strong believer, fulfilling all the basics of what God required of him according to the Jewish law. But deep in his heart, he didn't want to do the bare minimum. He wanted to give God more of his life. When Jesus reminded him to follow the Ten Commandments, the man remarkably replied, "All these I have observed; what do I still lack?" (Mt 19:20).

What a seemingly exceptional young man! Think about it: How many of us could say we are already following all of God's commandments? But that's not all. This man wasn't content with merely obeying all the rules — doing the right thing, saying the right thing, believing the right thing. He claimed he wanted to do even more for God. He wanted to give God his whole heart. So he asked Jesus, "What do I still lack?"

That's the same crucial question every true disciple should always ask: "What do I still lack?" How can I love more, serve more, trust more? How can I give more of my life to God? How can I live more like Jesus lived?

Being a disciple of Jesus is not about merely checking off boxes ("I prayed, I went to Mass, I led a Bible study, I didn't fall into mortal sin today"). It's not simply a matter of "doing the right things." Jesus invites us to give our entire lives to him. Being a disciple is ultimately about our total transformation in Christ — a lifelong process, but one that will never take off if we don't have the generous heart exhibited by this young man in Matthew 19.

DISCUSS

In what areas of your life are you currently striving for greater virtue, prayer, or friendship? In what ways are you trying to surrender more fully to God?

MORE THAN GOOD INTENTIONS

This young man in the Bible had noble aspirations. But sincere intentions are not enough. We have to put those intentions into action. Unfortunately, the story of this young man takes a downward turn after Jesus offers him this invitation: "If you would be perfect, go, sell what you possess and give to the poor, and you will have treasure in heaven; and come, follow me" (Mt 19:21). Instead of following where his generous heart has led him so far, the young man suddenly hesitates. He holds back. He has come a long way with his faith, and a part of him wants to go further — but this is one step he is unwilling to take. Instead of striving to give his entire life to Jesus, he went backwards in his faith journey and settled for mediocrity: "he went away sorrowful; for he had great possessions" (Mt 19:22).

Living as a disciple is a tall order. Jesus wants our whole hearts. He calls the rich young man and all of us to be holy as God is holy and to be perfect as the heavenly Father is perfect (Mt 5:48). Indeed, the goal of the Christian life is to be conformed to the image of Christ.

─────────────── **DISCUSS** ───────────────

Why do you think the rich young man refused to give up everything? Is there a part of your life that you are hesitant to give to Jesus?

AMAZING GRACE

But all this talk of perfection and holiness can be overwhelming. We might say to ourselves, "I have so many shortcomings, so many areas where I'm lacking! Is this really possible? Can I become holy as Christ is holy? Can I really become perfect?"

The answer is yes — but not in the way we might think. We are called to grow in virtue and holiness. But perfection is not achieved through a self-willed perfectionism. It's a transformation that can only take place through the power of God's grace.

"Grace" is a popular Christian word, but few understand what it truly means and what difference it makes in our daily lives. In essence, grace is Christ's divine life in us. It is the very life of the divine Son of God abiding in our souls!

We grow in grace through prayer, faithfulness, and most especially through the sacraments. By being filled with Christ's life, we are gradually changed and begin to think more like Christ. We begin to value what he values, serve more like him, bear sufferings more like him, love more like him — for it is Christ himself helping us to do things that we could not do on our own. Jesus wants to relive his life in us through grace.

To illustrate the power of grace in our souls, Catholics throughout the centuries have often used the image of a cold iron rod being placed in fire. As the fire heats the iron, the iron begins to take on the properties of the fire; it gets hot and glows red. The iron rod is still iron, but it becomes like the fire, even capable of igniting other fires. Through grace, something similar begins to happen in our lives. We are like the iron, placed in the fire of God's grace, becoming changed, taking on the characteristics of God — his love, patience, mercy, and kindness (Gal 5:22–23). The more we allow Christ's grace to transform us, the more we can say with St. Paul, "it is no longer I who live, but Christ who lives in me" (Gal 2:20).

We are not the sum of our weaknesses and failures; we are the sum of the Father's love for us and our real capacity to become the image of his Son.

— Pope St. John Paul II

Are you praying and striving for this type of transformation in your life? Do you call on God's grace to help you live more like Christ? Are you becoming more and more like God?

Imagine for a moment that you are meeting with someone who knows very little about Christianity. They want to understand Jesus and the Christian life, and so they decide to observe you. They notice how often you pray, how you treat your friends and family, the way you talk about other people, how hard you work, the shows you watch, the music you listen to, what you do on the weekends, how generous you are with your time, how well you care for those in need, how well you guard your purity — everything. After watching you for a month, would that person have a good idea of what it means to be a Christian? Or would they get a skewed, distorted image?

Be perfect as your heavenly Father is perfect.

— Matthew 5:48

There's a story of a peasant who traveled to Ars, France to see a famous priest named St. John Vianney. When the peasant returned home, his faith was renewed. Surprised, his friends and relatives asked him, "But who did you see in Ars?" He responded, "I saw God, in a man." People should be able to say the same about us.

DISCUSS

Like iron in the fire, how have you taken on some of the "properties" of God's love? Do you view your life as a disciple as being all about this process of transformation in Christ, or are you tempted to see being a disciple as an activity?

THREE ENEMIES: SELF-JUSTIFICATION, SELF-RELIANCE, SELF-CONDEMNATION

There are three things that keep us from taking on the character of Christ and growing in holiness.

- *Self-justification:* Like the rich young man in Matthew's Gospel, we convince ourselves that we don't need to make a lot of changes in our lives. We settle for where we are right now. We don't strive to give God more.

  Perhaps a part of us has sensed that we need to forgive someone, serve more, be more generous with our time, make a change, give up something, or stop doing something. But we're afraid — too attached, too set in our ways, too proud to reveal our weaknesses, too stubborn to admit we're wrong or too reluctant to give something up. What might we be tempted to do in these moments? We might rationalize our weaknesses and justify our lack of generous love. We tell ourselves we're doing better than most people — we pray, believe the Church's teachings, go to adoration, lead a Bible study. We're good enough. We don't really need to do more.

  In the end, this kind of self-justification is a way to cover up our spiritual laziness. It tries to hide the fact that we, like the rich young man, simply don't want to make the effort, sacrifices, and changes that deep friendship with Christ requires. Like the rich young man, we might practice our religion. But are we willing to offer ourselves completely as a gift to God?

- *Self-reliance:* Maybe you have tried to put your sins behind you before and follow Jesus completely. Or maybe you decided that you would never commit a certain sin again and have found yourself struggling and continuing to fall. Why does this happen?

  Sometimes God allows us to continue experiencing a certain weakness so that we grow in humility and become deeply

convinced of how incapable we are of conquering our sins on our own. As Fr. Jacques Philippe writes,

> We often have to experience failures, trials and humiliations, permitted by God, before this truth imposes itself on us, not only on an intellectual level, but as an experience of our entire being. God would spare us, if He could, all these trials, but they are necessary in order that we should be convinced of our complete powerlessness to do good by ourselves.[2]

We can easily forget how completely dependent we are on God for everything — most especially for rooting out sins and growing in holiness. Our transformation in Christ is impossible without the help of God's grace. If we try to rely on our own strength and follow our own timetables and plans for how we will achieve holiness, we are doomed to failure. Reflecting on her sinful past, St. Teresa of Avila wrote, "Self-reliance is what destroyed me."

Self-condemnation: When we face our sins and weaknesses, we might be tempted to get frustrated with ourselves or easily discouraged to see that we are not progressing in the spiritual life as we had hoped. We may say to ourselves, "I hate it when I do that! Why do I keep struggling with this? How come I'm not improving in this area?" Discouraging, self-condemning thoughts might enter our heads: "I'm so terrible. I'm never going to change! Why do I even bother trying?" Such thoughts, however, are not from God. They come from the enemy, the devil. He's the one whom the Bible calls "the accuser" (Rv 12:10).

Self-condemnation keeps us focused on ourselves and beaten down. It hinders us from turning to God with humble and contrite hearts. It keeps us from seeing our faults the way God sees them — not as the accuser, but as a loving Father who is "merciful and gracious, slow to anger, and abounding in steadfast love and faithfulness" (Ex 34:6).

DISCUSS

Which of these enemies do you struggle with the most? How can you seek to overcome them?

TAKE ACTION

Make a commitment to becoming more like Christ in one area of your life. Perhaps choose the area where you seem to struggle the most. Then, make a plan for the next few weeks detailing how you will grow to change this habit or strive to improve in this area of struggle. Consider:

- How will you encounter God's grace more deeply to help you conquer this struggle? What will you pray with? How will you let the sacraments build you up in this grace?

- What will need to change in your schedule? How will you spend your time differently?

- What kinds of accountability might you need to persevere in overcoming this struggle? To whom will you turn when you feel discouraged?

- How will you know that you have succeeded in becoming more like Christ? How will changing this habit or attaining this virtue allow you to love more freely and live more as a witness to Christ?

KEY CONCEPTS

"What do I still lack?": Unlike the rich young man in Matthew 19, disciples of Jesus should be willing to give up whatever stands in the way of a deeper friendship with Christ.

Grace: Christ's divine life in us

Iron in Fire Analogy: Just as iron takes on the properties of fire, so Christians through sanctifying grace take on the character of Christ.

ADDITIONAL RESOURCES

I Believe in Love: A Personal Retreat Based on the Teaching of St. Thérèse of Lisieux by Fr. Jean C. B. d'Elbee

Searching for and Maintaining Peace by Jacques Philippe

Back to Virtue: Traditional Moral Wisdom for Modern Moral Confusion by Peter Kreeft

The Imitation of Christ by Thomas à Kempis

Notes

Notes

[1] Jean-Baptiste Chautard, *The Soul of the Apostolate* (Charlotte, NC: TAN Books, 1946), 122.

[2] Jacques Philippe, *Searching for and Maintaining Peace: A Small Treatise on Peace of Heart* (Staten Island, NY: Alba House, 2002), 4.

6.1

DEEPER PRAYER

PERSEVERING IN LOVE

Optional *Lectio Divina* Prayer

1. Read Ephesians 1:3–14.
2. Meditate on the words.
3. Speak to Christ about this passage.
4. Rest and listen in God's presence.
5. Discuss together.

Teresa of Jesus, barefoot and determined, set out on a journey.

Her mission? To bring the Carmelite convents of Spain back to their founding principles of poverty, silence, and penance after years of lax spiritual practices and worldliness throughout the order.

Many who knew Teresa in her early days in the convent would have been surprised by the zealous reformer she had become. Teresa Sanchez de Cepeda y Ahumada entered the prestigious Carmelite convent in Avila at twenty-one years of age. Beautiful, intelligent, and charming, the outgoing Teresa was not as comfortable in the quiet solitude of the chapel, but preferred the thriving social life of the parlor, where visitors of high social and political rank frequently entertained the sisters with meaningless conversations, distracting them from their spiritual practices. Teresa struggled through her required periods of prayer, even saying at one point, "I don't know what heavy penance I would not have gladly undertaken rather than practice prayer."

For twenty years, Teresa half-heartedly pursued the contemplative life of her order. But one day, when she was nearly forty years old, Teresa experienced a profound conversion after seeing a statue of the suffering Jesus and realizing "how poorly [she] had thanked him for those wounds."[1] That experience shook her prayer life to its core, and she began pursuing a deeper union with Jesus with renewed discipline and love.

Seeing with new eyes the lukewarm practices in the Carmelites all around her, Teresa was moved to inspire her sisters to re-commit to daily silent prayer and penance. Despite facing much opposition, Teresa went on to found seventeen new convents, and young women flocked to them. An active reformer, Teresa traveled, wrote, and taught frequently — but all throughout her efforts, she never allowed her work to keep her from prayer. She discovered that "prayer and comfortable living are incompatible."[2]

For twenty years, Teresa settled for a dry, distracted, and inconsistent

prayer life that produced very little fruit. But after her conversion, her deep commitment to the spiritual life transformed everyone around her: her community, her religious order and, eventually, the entire Church. St. Teresa of Avila was declared a Doctor of the Church in 1970. The sister who resisted prayer became a great saint of the interior life. Like her, if we want to share Christ with the world, we need to be people who are willing to persevere in the journey of prayer.

―――――――――――――― **DISCUSS** ――――――――――――――

What about St. Teresa's story is inspiring or convicting to you? How has your prayer life deepened or changed in the last six months?

SOUL OF THE APOSTOLATE

As St. Teresa of Avila's life demonstrates, mission and conversion are the fruit of a deep and disciplined life of prayer. The more a heart is immersed in the life of Christ, the more fruitful each missionary action can be. One bishop said of Teresa and her order, "Ten Carmelite nuns praying will be of greater help to me than twenty missionaries preaching."[3] In the same way, our outreach efforts will only be effective to the extent that they are born out of deep, committed daily prayer.

Jesus himself makes this clear in John 15:5: "Apart from me, you can do nothing." He did not say "apart from me, you can do some things" or "without me, you'll just be a little less successful." Jesus makes clear that our actions, even those done for the good of his kingdom, will be fruitless without his grace.

Unfortunately, sometimes we become so busy with projects and activities in service of God's work that we don't allow him to be the true source of our missionary efforts. St. Bernard describes this difficulty, using the images of reservoirs and channels:

> The channels let the water flow away, and do not retain a drop. But the reservoir is first filled, and then, without emptying itself, pours out its overflow, which is ever renewed, over the fields which it waters. How many there are that are devoted to works, who are never anything but channels, and retain nothing for themselves, but remain dry while trying to pass on life-giving grace to souls! We have many channels in the Church today, but very few reservoirs.[4]

We need to be filled with Christ's love to share it with anyone else. To pursue a life of mission without first being filled up by grace is to allow our hearts to remain dry and untransformed. As we enter more deeply into mission, the temptation will be to fill our schedule with meetings over coffee, events at our parish, and other outreach activities, leaving less and less time to pray and participate in the sacraments. It can be tempting to think that we are being successful evangelists in this way. However, "we must never leave the God of works for the works of God."[5]

DISCUSS

Looking at your current prayer life, are you more like a channel or a reservoir? Do you struggle with the temptation to choose activities over time for prayer, the sacraments, and spiritual formation?

CHASING A FEELING

If we hope to lead others to Jesus, we need to first be deeply rooted in him ourselves. But maybe you've felt the frustration in your heart: "I know that prayer is important, but right now, it's just difficult! Prayer feels boring, and, sometimes, I just want to be anywhere else other than alone with Jesus in prayer. I want to share his love with others, but how can I do that if I don't *feel* like I am being filled?"

The spiritual life is full of highs and lows, and you will encounter times when prayer is difficult, dry, or boring. But the truth remains that Jesus shows up every time we pray, and the success of our prayer does not depend on how strongly we "feel" his presence. Being faithful to God each day in prayer is much more important than any feelings of his closeness we might experience in prayer.

St. John of the Cross describes the desire for an emotional experience of God in prayer as "spiritual gluttony." What does this mean? We can be tempted to crave consolations and emotions as proof of the effectiveness of our prayer. We do things to try to spark that feeling of God's closeness, and we get frustrated or discouraged when the feelings aren't there. St. John has strong words for those seeking such things:

> "They think the whole matter of prayer consists in looking for sensory satisfaction. When they do not get this sensible comfort, they become very disconsolate and think they have done nothing. All their time is spent looking for satisfaction and spiritual consolation; one minute they are meditating on one subject and the next on another, always in search for some gratification of the things of God."[6]

Are we coming to prayer to praise, honor, and love our King? Or are we coming to get something from him, some insight or emotion? As we mature in prayer, Jesus sometimes takes away some of the consolations, delights, or ease of prayer — not because he never wants us to have these, but because he is purifying us, increasing our desire for him alone. He is also testing our hearts: Will we remain faithful to him in prayer even if the feelings aren't there? Our closest friends are people who love us for who we are, not for what we do for them. That's the kind of friendship the Lord wants with us: a deep friendship based not on how he makes us feel, but for who he is.

------------------------- **DISCUSS** -------------------------

Do you find yourself falling into spiritual gluttony in your prayer life? Do you judge the success of your prayer by how you feel? How have you sought to love God for his sake, not just for the delights he gives?

THE STRUGGLE OF PRAYER

The *Catechism*'s description of prayer can be a helpful truth to ponder as we navigate struggles in prayer: "[P]rayer is a battle. Against whom? Against ourselves and against the wiles of the tempter who does all he can to turn man away from prayer, away from union with God ... The 'spiritual battle' of the Christian's new life is inseparable from the battle of prayer" (CCC 2725).

What are the common struggles you experience in the battle of prayer? Does prayer feel **dry**, boring, or uninteresting? Are you experiencing **discouragement** in your prayer journey or feeling tempted to believe that the Lord is far from you? Are you **distracted** and having a difficult time staying focused in prayer? Are you having trouble keeping the prayer commitments you have made?

When these struggles occur, there are actions we can take to overcome them.

In prayer we must not seek the consolations of God, but the God of consolations.

— St. Francis de Sales

> *The most essential thing is that we should love God without any motive of self-interest.*
>
> — St. Teresa of Avila

Examine: One important step is to examine our lives and to see if there is anything preventing us from praying well. Are you getting enough sleep? Is your schedule a source of distraction? Are you choosing a time or a place to pray that keeps you from entering deeply into prayer? Do you turn you phone off during prayer? Is there a sin in your heart that you are avoiding bringing to the Lord? Noticing the areas of our physical and spiritual lives that may be an obstacle to our prayer can help us make necessary changes.

Accept the Invitation to Go Deeper: Dryness in prayer is an invitation to go deeper. Think of a child who is just learning to walk. In the beginning, they need their parents to hold their hands as they learn how to take steps. Eventually, however, the parent begins to let go, allowing the child to walk on their own. In prayer, consolations can be like God holding our hands to get us started. But as we grow, he begins to let go — not so that we fall, but so that we can learn to go even further in our relationship with him.

Offer It Up: Offer your discouragement to God. These little sufferings can be a source of grace for our lives and the lives of others when we unite our struggles to Jesus on the cross. By doing this, we can turn our dryness in prayer into powerful intercession for others.

Persevere and Trust: All Christians experience struggles in prayer. These are not a sign of unworthiness or that God has abandoned us. Trust that God is working, even when things are dry, and persevere through the difficulty. When prayer gets hard, we can be tempted to give up, but that's exactly what the enemy wants us to do. Keep showing up, persevere in your prayer commitments, and do not panic when it gets difficult. Instead, turn to the Lord and trust that he is working.

Seek Help: Another good step to take in times of struggle in prayer is to seek help from a trusted spiritual mentor or spiritual director. We can be tempted to keep quiet about our struggles in prayer so that we don't seem weak, but seeking help is a great way to remove obstacles and receive guidance and encouragement.

DISCUSS

Are you experiencing any of these struggles in your prayer life? In what ways is the enemy trying to draw you away from prayer? Which of these steps do you need to take to pursue a deeper relationship with Christ?

TAKE ACTION

Take five minutes and make one or two resolutions for your own prayer life. What do you need to change with your prayer so that the Lord can fill your heart and his love can overflow to others? How will you deal with the struggles you are facing in prayer? When and how will you make these changes?

KEY CONCEPTS

Soul of the Apostolate: Without a deep commitment to daily prayer, our apostolic work will not be fruitful.

Spiritual Gluttony: We should not chase feelings in prayer but should seek the Lord for who he is, not how he makes us feel.

ADDITIONAL RESOURCES

Soul of the Apostolate by Dom Jean-Baptiste Chautard

CCC 2725–2745: "The Battle of Prayer"

The Discernment of Spirits: An Ignatian Guide for Everyday Living by. Fr. Timothy Gallagher

Introduction to the Devout Life by St. Francis de Sales

Worshipping a Hidden God by Archbishop Luis M. Martinez

The Power of Silence Against a Dictatorship of Noise by Robert Cardinal Sarah

Notes

Notes

¹ St. Teresa of Avila, *The Autobiography of St. Teresa of Avila: The Life of Teresa of Jesus*, trans. David Lewis (Rockford, IL: TAN Books, 1997), 65.

² St. Teresa of Avila, *The Way of Perfection*, trans. Kieran Kavanaugh, O.C.D. and Otilio Rodriguez, O.C.D. (Washington, D.C., ICS Publications, 2000), Chapter 4, para. 2.

³ Jean-Baptiste Chautard, *The Soul of the Apostolate* (Charlotte, NC: TAN Books, 1946).

⁴ Ibid.

⁵ Ibid.

⁶ St. John of the Cross, *Dark Night of the Soul* (New York: Image Books, 1959), 175.

6.2

WORKS OF MERCY

Optional *Lectio Divina* Prayer

1. Read Matthew 25:31–46.
2. Meditate on the words.
3. Speak to Christ about this passage.
4. Rest and listen in God's presence.
5. Discuss together.

There's no skyline in Calcutta, India.

In contrast to India's beautiful countryside, a polluted haze blurs the cityscape. Poor people line every curb of the sprawling metropolis. Make no mistake: Calcutta is not a comfortable place. Nevertheless, it is the city Mother Teresa called home.

Why spend a lifetime in Calcutta? Mother Teresa could have lived anywhere, so why choose to stay in this city?

It was fascination with this choice that motivated a young man named Bill to spend his summer serving with Mother Teresa's sisters, the Missionaries of Charity. Bill was not a practicing Christian but was moved to work at Mother Teresa's famous "Home for the Dying," a primitive hospice designed to give the poor in Calcutta a place to die with dignity.

Bill's job was unique. The sisters needed a volunteer to leave each morning and find those who were dying and had no one to care for them. As a strong, twenty-one-year-old male, Bill seemed like a perfect candidate. Each morning he would leave the hospice center in search of the many dying individuals who were rejected by their own family and friends, literally thrown away and left to die alone on the city streets. He quickly discovered that his search was most fruitful near Calcutta's busy train stations. In the surrounding villages, the unwanted would be put on a train with a one-way ticket to Calcutta, where they would be thrown out and left to die on their own near the tracks instead of being cared for by their children, siblings, family, or friends.

Searching for bodies next to the screeching locomotives, Bill would find the dying huddled along the platforms. He would then carry them back to the sisters. Some lived. Most died in a matter of weeks. Others didn't make it even that long. And some were dead by the time Bill found their corpses in the gutters.

Whatever you did for one of these least brothers of mine, you did for me.

— *Matthew 25:40*

Why would Mother Teresa choose to remain in this city, where the streets resembled a poor man's coffin? After working for a month, Bill was even more confounded than when he began. "Calcutta's gutters are no home," he thought to himself. "They're graveyards!" Bill did not understand Mother's decision until one afternoon a fellow volunteer recounted an old story:

> One day Mother told us of a man who lay dying in a gutter, half-eaten by worms, rotting. She carried him herself to the home for the sick and dying. She laid him in a bed, washed his entire body using a basin and cloth, picked the maggots out of his open wounds and dressed them with ointment, laid him in fresh sheets, and gave him a drink of cold water. He was given what he had not known until then: a clean place to lie, unconditional love, and dignity. "I have lived like an animal all my life," the man told her, "but I will die like an angel."[1]

Why would Mother Teresa do all this for a dying man she just met? Because he is Jesus to her. As Mother Teresa herself once explained, "I see Jesus in every human being. I say to myself, this is hungry Jesus, I must feed him. This is sick Jesus. This one has leprosy or gangrene; I must wash him and tend to him. I serve because I love Jesus."[2]

With this background, everything suddenly clicked for Bill. He had come to Calcutta wanting to do some "good service," approaching the poor as a project to be completed. For him, each poor person was a task to be checked off his list. Mother Teresa approached things differently. Her ministry was much more than a social program; it was a place of encounter. Why did Mother stay in Calcutta? Because this is where she was called to encounter Jesus: in the unwanted, rejected, abandoned poor. For her, Jesus lived in the gutters. When she looked at a poor, dying man, the Lord of the Universe looked back.

Notes

--- **DISCUSS** ---

How does Mother Teresa's example change how you understand serving the poor?

THE POOR, OUR BROTHERS AND SISTERS

The Catholic Church has been called "the world's biggest charity" with more than 140,000 schools, 10,000 orphanages, 5,000 hospitals, and some 16,000 other health clinics around the globe.[3] But what's behind this tradition? Is helping the poor simply "the right thing to do" or a way to be a nice person, or is there a deeper meaning to the Church's practice of helping those in need?

In Matthew 25, Jesus tells a parable that unveils the deeper reason for our care for the poor. He tells a parable on the Last Judgment in which all people will be separated into two groups at the end of time.

One group inherits the kingdom because they helped Jesus when he was in need; the other group does not. With some confusion, the righteous ask, "Lord, when did we see you hungry and feed you, or thirsty and give you drink? When did we see you a stranger and welcome you, or naked and clothe you? When did we see you ill or in prison, and visit you?" (Mt 25:37–39).

> *The biggest disease in the West today is the feeling of being unwanted, unloved and uncared for.*
>
> — St. Mother Teresa

Our Lord answers them, "Amen, I say to you, whatever you did for one of these least brothers of mine, you did for me" (Mt 25:40). In contrast, the parable notes that those who did not help the poor will not inherit the kingdom.

In this passage, Jesus forces us to rethink how we view the poor. When we serve the poor, we grow deeper in our divine intimacy with our Lord because when we encounter them, we encounter Jesus himself. Jesus invites us to "recognize his own presence in the poor who are his brethren" (CCC 2449). Pope Francis has said, "We must learn how to be with the poor, to share with those who lack basic necessities, to touch the flesh of Christ! The Christian is not one who speaks about the poor, no! He is one who encounters them, who looks them in the eye, who touches them."[4]

DISCUSS

If you were to face Jesus today, what do you think he would say to you based on how you have treated the poor?

CATHOLIC SOCIAL TEACHING: WORKS OF MERCY LIVED OUT

The world faces many forms of poverty, both material and spiritual. Pope Benedict XVI once said, "The deepest poverty is the inability of joy, the tediousness of a life considered absurd and contradictory. This poverty is widespread today, in very different forms in the materially rich as well as the poor countries."[5] The poor, therefore, includes both the person who is hungry and homeless and the person who is well off financially but whose life is plagued by loneliness, emptiness, and meaninglessness.

We don't have to go all the way to Calcutta, India, to find the poor and suffering. They are all around us: in our city, at our parish, in our workplace, on our campus, in our families. For those who have eyes to see, there are not only many people suffering from physical ailments and material poverty, but also many who feel unwanted, unloved, and unknown, and still many others who suffer from loneliness, fear, anxiety, and various forms of emotional and psychological wounds and illnesses. Will we make it a priority to care for them?

Notes

As in the early Church, one of the greatest signs of being a faithful Christian today is caring for the poor. In other words, if you want to know if you are a faithful disciple of Jesus, you must not only pray, frequent the sacraments, follow the teachings of the Church, and live a moral life. All that, of course, is essential. But you also must care for the poor, love those who are suffering, and work toward eliminating poverty in all its forms. In a self-centered, individualistic age which prompts us to be focused on our own comfort, interests, and pleasure, Christians who get out of themselves and serve the poor, the addicted, the elderly, the immigrant, the lonely, and the unborn are, according to Pope Francis, "a prophetic, counter-cultural resistance" to the self-centered lifestyles promoted in secular culture today.[6]

And when we do care for the poor, we not only make a difference out in the world, but something also profoundly changes within us. We begin to participate more deeply in Christ's own love, compassion, generosity, and kindness. We begin to take on the heart of Christ. How can we serve the poor around us? How can we show them mercy? The Church has traditionally recommended what it calls the seven corporal and seven spiritual works of mercy:

Corporal Works of Mercy	*Spiritual Works of Mercy*
Feeding the hungry	Instructing the ignorant
Giving drink to the thirsty	Counseling the doubtful
Clothing the naked	Admonishing the sinner
Offering hospitality to the homeless	Bearing wrongs patiently
Visiting the imprisoned	Forgiving offenses willingly
Caring for the sick	Comforting the afflicted
Burying the dead	Praying for the living and the dead

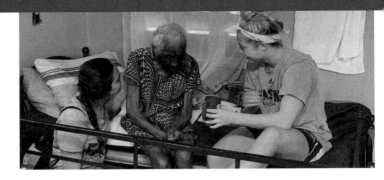

DISCUSS

Where do you observe poverty in your life right now? After reading the corporal and spiritual works of mercy, how might God be calling you to share his mercy with the world?

TAKE ACTION

As you contemplate how you can incorporate the works of mercy into your life, ask yourself, "What can I do to begin to serve the poor around me?" Then, make a commitment to do something. You may not be able to solve every example of poverty you encounter, but God is inviting you to do something. For more ideas, see the list at the end of this article. You might also consider going on a FOCUS mission trip.

Additionally, come up with creative ways for making the works of mercy part of your efforts toward evangelization. Whom could you bring with you to serve the poor, and how might that experience help them come to know Jesus Christ in a deeper way?

KEY CONCEPTS

We are all called to love Jesus in the poor and suffering: "Whatever you did for one of these least brothers of mine, you did for me" (Mt 25:40, NAB).

Corporal and Spiritual Works of Mercy: Christian disciples should care for those suffering in material poverty (the poor, the sick, etc.) and those afflicted by various spiritual forms of poverty (such as loneliness, emotional hurts, not knowing Christ, etc.).

ADDITIONAL RESOURCES

From the FOCUS Blog on focusequip.org: "50 Corporal Works of Mercy Ideas for Your Summer Bucket List" by Lisa Cotter

Saints and Social Justice by Brandon Vogt

No Greater Love by Mother Teresa, Ch. 4: "On Poverty & the Poor"

Charity: The Place of the Poor in the Biblical Tradition by Gary Anderson

Notes

[1] Barbara J. Elliot, "When Mother Teresa Came to Washington," *The Imaginative Conservative*, accessed March 27, 2019, https://theimaginativeconservative.org/2016/09/mother-teresa-came-washington-barbara-j-elliott.html.

[2] Justina Miller, "Mother Teresa: each one of them is Jesus in disguise," *Pureflix*, accessed March 27, 2019, https://insider.pureflix.com/news/mother-teresa-each-one-of-them-is-jesus-in-disguise.

[3] David Paton, "The World's Biggest Charity," *Catholic Herald*, accessed March 27, 2019, https://catholicherald.co.uk/issues/february-17th-2017/a-worldwide-force-for-good/.

[4] Francis, "Meeting with the Poor Assisted by Caritas, Address of Pope Francis," accessed March 30, 2020, Vatican.va.

[5] Cardinal Joseph Ratzinger, "Address of Cardinal Joseph Ratzinger on the Jubilee of Catechists and Religion Teachers (December 10, 2000)," accessed April 2, 2020, https://d2y1pz2y630308.cloudfront.net/5032/documents/2014/0/ADDRESS%20TO%20CATECHISTS%20AND%20RELIGION%20TEACHERS.pdf

[6] Francis, *Evangelii Gaudium*, accessed April 2, 2020, Vatican.va, 193.

[7] Lisa Cotter, "50 Corporal Works of Mercy Ideas for Your Summer Bucket List," *FOCUS Blog*, July 3, 2017, https://focusoncampus.org/content/50-corporal-works-of-mercy-ideas-for-your-summer-bucket-list.

INTERCESSORY PRAYER

Optional *Lectio Divina* Prayer

1. Read Luke 5:18–26.
2. Meditate on the words.
3. Speak to Christ about this passage.
4. Rest and listen in God's presence.
5. Discuss together.

I n 1887, France was gripped by a murder mystery involving the grisly deaths of three women in Paris.

After the investigation had taken several twists and turns, the police arrested Henri Pranzini, a known criminal with a sordid past. Pranzini denied the triple murder and tried to provide an alibi, but the evidence gradually mounted against him. His trial lasted just five days and, at its conclusion, Pranzini was found guilty and sentenced to death by guillotine.

Despite the evidence, Pranzini showed no remorse or shame. He refused to repent of his past life or of the crime he committed. On the morning of his execution, a chaplain came to his cell to offer confession. With bravado, Pranzini walked past the priest and up to the scaffold to face his death. As he arrived, he changed his mind; he turned to the priest, asked for a crucifix and kissed Jesus' wounds three times as a sign of faith and repentance.

While all of France was fascinated by the fate of Pranzini, one fourteen-year-old girl took a particular interest in the case. Upon hearing of Pranzini's death sentence, she felt a specific call to pray for the man so that his soul did not fall into hell. While she was confident that God would hear her prayer no matter what, she asked for a sign, even a small one, to show her that her prayer was answered. While we'll never know the full story, Pranzini's kiss of the crucifix seemed to be a sign that the prayer of this fourteen-year-old girl — later known as St. Thérèse of Lisieux — was answered.

Thérèse's intercessory prayers for others was one of the hallmarks of her life. She prayed not only for lost souls like Pranzini and people around the world who did not know Christ, but she also always prayed for family members, religious sisters in her convent, and the novices entrusted to her care. She had a specific mission of fervently praying, fasting, and making sacrifices for missionary priests, empowering their work in evangelization to bear much fruit and help save souls. One of these priests wrote to Thérèse's convent asking for a nun to pray for his soul and his mission.

Thérèse responded, "Let us work together for the salvation of souls. We have only the one day of this life to save them and thus to give Our Lord some proof of our love."[1]

Thérèse has continued her mission of interceding for others while in heaven. Shortly after her death, her autobiography, *Story of a Soul*, was printed and distributed in France, then in Europe, and then through the whole world. Over time, hundreds of letters poured into Thérèse's convent, telling of the miracles that occurred through the intercession of this incredible saint. In 1927, just thirty years after her death, Pope Pius XI named this powerful intercessor the patroness of missions.

DISCUSS

St. Thérèse had an incredible desire to win souls through her intercession in prayer. Do you have this same desire to intercede for others? What is your current experience with intercessory prayer? Do you feel comfortable sharing the power of this prayer method with others?

A VISION FOR INTERCESSORY PRAYER

The *Catechism* says that intercessory prayer "consists in asking on behalf of another" (CCC 2647). What kind of power does this prayer hold? As Pope Francis tells us, "Intercession is like a 'leaven' in the heart of the Trinity. It is a way of penetrating the Father's heart and discovering new dimensions which can shed light on concrete situations and change them."[2]

When we practice intercessory prayer, we imitate our Lord. While on Earth, Jesus prayed for others, and he continues to be an advocate for us in heaven. As Hebrews 7:25 tells us, "He is able for all time to save those who draw near to God through him, since he always lives to make intercession for them."

Not only does Jesus intercede for us, but he also responds to our intercessory prayers for others. In Luke Chapter 5, we see what happens when people bring the needs of their friends to Jesus.

The crowds are beginning to follow Jesus because they hear of his healings. Several men carry their paralytic friend up to be healed by Jesus, but they can't reach him through the crowds. Unwilling to be stopped, they lowered him through a hole they had made in the roof tiles. What happens next tells us something incredibly important about the power of intercessory prayer: "And when [Jesus] saw their faith he said, 'Man, your sins are forgiven'" (Lk 5:20). Notice how Jesus forgives the man because of the faith of his friends.

When we love and intercede for each other, the Father delights; it opens his heart and moves him to respond. The faith of this group of friends is what moves Jesus to action. They loved their friend so much that they were willing to work and sacrifice to bring him to Jesus. Are you willing to do the same for the people in your life? You know people who are suffering, who don't know Christ, or who are not practicing the Catholic Faith. Do you bring them to Jesus through your fervent prayers for them? If Jesus sees your faith, he may work a miracle in their lives.

Notes

> *Prayer is the best weapon we have; it is the key to God's heart.*
>
> — *St. Padre Pio*

DISCUSS

Do you believe that your personal prayers can actually make an impact in the lives of others? What, if anything, holds you back from being open to the Holy Spirit in this way?

GETTING STARTED

Most of us know that intercessory prayer is important. Unfortunately, sometimes it can become just a "good idea" or something we do sporadically, whenever someone comes to mind. However, it's important to make it a part of our lives each day. Throughout the

history of the Church, intercessory prayer has played a vital role in the work of saving souls. As missionary disciples, we ought to spend time every day talking to God about people and spend the rest of the day talking to people about God.

To do this, we must come to prayer with the right disposition and build up good habits of praying for others. Let's look at a few key truths about prayer and try and build this habit in our lives.

Dispositions in Prayer

As you consider praying for others, here are some things to keep in mind as you prepare to pray:

- God truly hears our prayers. Don't underestimate how vital and powerful your prayers can be.

- This is God's work. The Holy Spirit is the principal agent of evangelization. When we intercede for others, we allow him to do the heavy lifting in our work of bringing souls closer to Christ.

- Have confidence in God. Our reliance on God in prayer banishes fear and allows us to place situations and people in his hands. Sometimes we feel small, weak, and helpless, but all our requests and feelings can be given over to him.

You pay God a compliment by asking great things of him.

— St. Teresa of Avila

- Be humble. We don't come to God with our list of expectations, which he must then fulfill. We come to him with trust, like children coming to their parents. In fact, interceding for others should lead us to be less self-centered as we step outside of ourselves and consider the needs of others.

- Pray specifically. Pray boldly. What do you want God to do? Don't feel like your prayer needs to be couched in pious language. Share your heart honestly with God. And don't think anything is too big for God. Often, we ask for too little, not too much!

Practices of Intercessory Prayer

Intercessory prayer can take many different forms. Each time you go to Mass, you can offer it for a particular person or intention. You might consider gathering a group of people together and praying out loud for the needs of others. You could even make little sacrifices, like not putting cream in your coffee or drinking only water, as prayers for people's needs. The ways we can intercede for others are endless. Here are a few practical ideas to consider:

- Write down people's names and pray for their needs daily.

- Imagine the people you want to pray for in your own mind or place their pictures somewhere near where you pray. Seeing their faces can motivate you to pray for them more specifically and more regularly.

- Pray with others in person. Your prayer doesn't have to be alone and in silence. It's great to pray for people when you are with them. Be sure to get their permission first, ask them what they need prayers for and then pray out loud for their needs. Praying in this way can be very powerful. Instead of just saying "I'll pray for you," they get to hear your prayer right away in that moment.

Notes

- Pray at specific locations. Maybe it's where you have Bible study; maybe it's a place that needs conversion; maybe it's a room where you study, work, or teach: All of these places are great reminders to intercede for others daily. By praying in specific places, you ask for God's blessing upon all who enter there.

- Pray as you plan. Our work should be God's work, first and foremost. Therefore, whenever we begin an apostolic task, we should ask for God's guidance and blessing on all we are about to do.

- Consider offering up some sort of fast or penance alongside your prayer for others. Jesus himself notes the spiritual power of prayer paired with fasting (Mk 9:29), and St. Paul describes the value of offering up our suffering for the Body of Christ: "I rejoice in my sufferings for your sake, and in my flesh I complete what is lacking in Christ's afflictions for the sake of his body, that is, the Church" (Col 1:24).

DISCUSS

What keeps you from praying for others more often? How can you make intercessory prayer a daily habit in your life?

TAKE ACTION

One simple way to get started praying for others is to write down some names and to start praying! You can use your Prayer and Accompaniment Chart (pg. 159) to help you get started. As you recognize where people in your life are on the journey of missionary discipleship, you can pray for them more specifically and intentionally. This tool is a great way to keep those you are accompanying lifted up in prayer.

After you write down a few names, take some time right now to pray for someone. Feel free to use some of practical suggestions in the article. Intercede for this person and ask for the Lord to work powerfully in their life.

KEY CONCEPTS

Intercessory Prayer: Modeled by Jesus and the saints, praying for others is a key part of the Christian life (Heb 7:25; 2 Tm 1:3; CCC 2634–36).

Intercession and Missionary Discipleship: Missionary disciples ought to spend time every day talking to God about people and spend the rest of their day talking to people about God.

ADDITIONAL RESOURCES

CCC 2634–2636: "Prayer of Intercession"

Notes

[1] Patrick Ahern, *Maurice and Therese: The Story of a Love* (New York: Image Books, 2001).

[2] Francis, *Evangelii Gaudium,* accessed March 30, 2020, Vatican.va, 283.

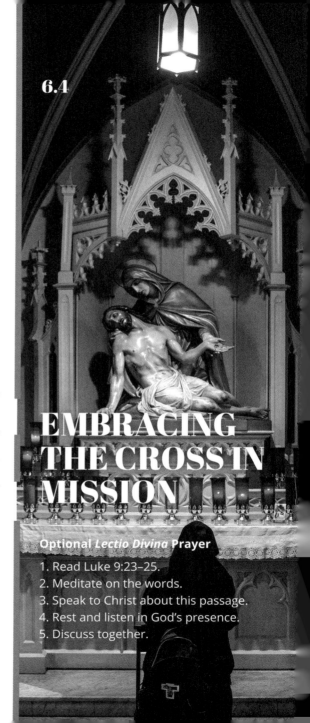

6.4

"TAKE UP YOUR CROSS AND FOLLOW ME"

EMBRACING THE CROSS IN MISSION

Optional *Lectio Divina* Prayer

1. Read Luke 9:23–25.
2. Meditate on the words.
3. Speak to Christ about this passage.
4. Rest and listen in God's presence.
5. Discuss together.

I magine Jesus looking you in the eye and saying the following words:

Notes

"If any man would come after me, let him deny himself and take up his cross daily and follow me" (Lk 9:23).

"Whoever does not bear his own cross and come after me, cannot be my disciple" (Lk 14:27).

Those are the stark words Jesus spoke to the original disciples. And it floored them. Pick up your cross?

Christians today have a comfortable familiarity with the image of the cross: We have crosses in our churches, some people have crosses hanging in their homes, and some even wear crosses as jewelry around their necks. But that was certainly not the case in Jesus' day. In fact, in the first-century Roman world, the whole idea of the cross was completely abhorrent. The cross was the Roman Empire's most dreadful instrument of torture, humiliation, and execution. The famous ancient Roman orator Cicero once said, "The very word 'cross' should be far removed not only from the person of a Roman citizen but from his thoughts, his eyes, and his ears."[1] You didn't even want to *think* about the cross.

That's what makes Jesus' statement so startling. For Jesus to tell his disciples to pick up a cross and follow him would have been as shocking as him telling people in the modern world to pick up their electric chairs or pick up their guillotines and follow him. Of all the images Jesus could have used to depict discipleship, why would he choose this most horrific one? Noah got a rainbow. Moses got a burning bush. The Magi got a star in the sky. Why do Jesus' disciples get a cross?

Because, as we will see, it's only through the cross that we find our ultimate fulfillment in life and experience what we're made for: the total, perfect, self-giving love of God himself.

--- **DISCUSS** ---

Considering this first-century understanding of the cross, what do you think the apostles were thinking when they heard Jesus tell them that, if they wanted to be his disciple, they had to pick up the cross and follow him? What would you have been thinking? Would this have made you hesitate or reconsider your call as a disciple? Why or why not?

MADE FOR LOVE

When you are on mission for the Gospel, you should expect trials, roadblocks, obstacles, rejection. Don't be surprised when mission requires a lot of your time and energy, when people misunderstand you, when people turn down your invitations or turn away from the Gospel. All this happened to Jesus, so you shouldn't expect anything less. After all, Jesus promised the cross, not comfort. *But why?*

It all has to do with his love. For Jesus, the cross is much more than a form of execution. It's ultimately his fullest revelation of God's inner life, which is all about total self-giving love: "God is love" (1 Jn 4:8). For all eternity, the Father loves the Son and gives himself totally to the Son. The Son in return loves the Father, giving of himself completely to the Father, holding nothing back. And this bond of love between the Father and the Son is the Third Person of the Trinity, the Holy Spirit. God's inner life as the Trinity is all about perfect, infinite, self-giving love.

But what happens when the Eternal Son of God enters time and space and takes on human flesh in Jesus Christ? He continues doing what he has done for all eternity: giving himself in love totally to the Father. But in Christ, the Son's infinite divine love is now expressed in finite human nature. That's like putting a rubber balloon up to a water hydrant: the balloon is going to explode. When infinite love expresses itself in our limited, finite humanity, it will involve suffering, sacrifice, death: "Greater love has no man than this, that a man lay down his life for his friends" (Jn 15:13).

Through the cross, God reveals himself most fully, his very inner life, which is love. And in the process, he shows us what we're all made for. The God who is love made us in his own image and likeness. We, therefore, are made to live like God, which involves *loving like God loves*. So much did God desire to make this clear for us that he took on human flesh in Jesus Christ and showed us what his perfect love looks like: total self-giving love. That's what we're made for. We are made for the cross. In other words, we are made to give our lives completely as a gift like Jesus did for us on Calvary.

Jesus himself said, "unless a grain of wheat falls into the earth and dies, it remains alone; but if it dies, it bears much fruit. He who loves his life loses it, and he who hates his life in this world will keep it for eternal life" (Jn 12:24–25).

This is the law of self-giving. Written in the fabric of our being is this great mystery of self-giving love: When we give of ourselves in love to God, to mission and to others, we don't lose anything, but our lives are deeply enriched and we gain so much more, for we are living according to the way God made us. Indeed, we are living like God himself, in whose image we have been created. That's why the Church teaches that "man ... cannot fully find himself except through a sincere gift of himself."[2] In other words, it's only when we live like the God-man, Jesus Christ, giving our lives to God and to others in sacrificial love, that we will find our true happiness in life.

—————————————— **DISCUSS** ——————————————

Why is self-giving love so important? How have you lived this out in your own life? What were the effects?

THE CROSS: THE NEXT LEVEL OF DISCIPLESHIP

The Gospels tell us that great multitudes came out to see Jesus throughout his public ministry. Many were excited about his dynamic preaching. Many others followed him from village to village because they were amazed by his miracles. Still others sought Jesus because he could heal their loved ones who were sick. But few were willing to commit and remain close to him when things got hard, when it required radical trust and sacrifice (Mt 8:19ff). The lack of true disciples became clear on Good Friday. While there were large crowds impressed by the many signs and wonders Jesus offered throughout his public ministry, they were nowhere to be seen on Calvary. Only a very small group of followers remained with Jesus in his greatest hour of need. The crowds in Jerusalem on that day instead were shouting out, "Crucify him, crucify him!" (Jn 19:6).

When we first start growing in friendship with God, we, like the crowds, often are attracted to what God does for us — the benefits of living a Christian life (better friends, peace, help with problems, a sense of purpose, etc.) or the graces God gives. But as we mature in faith, God invites us to go to the next level of discipleship, the next level of love. He invites us to give ourselves to him completely, to love him and serve him for his own sake, not just because of what he does for us. He invites us to love like Jesus loves: unconditionally, expecting nothing in return, all the way to the cross. That is the type of discipleship to which we are called.

The devil, however, hates it when Christians start to love in this radical way, especially when they are committed to the work of evangelization. When he sees souls starting to take that next level of self-giving love and discipleship, he tempts them to pursue instead a *self-seeking* love — to seek what is most interesting, comfortable, enjoyable, or advantageous. Instead of living Christlike, sacrificial love and seeking opportunities to truly live for God and for others, the devil tempts us to run away from the cross and live for self.

When we face these temptations of the enemy, it is important to view the challenges in our lives not as problems to be solved or as difficulties to be avoided at all costs, but rather to view them from a supernatural perspective: as opportunities to meet Jesus in those challenges and to grow in love and trust of him. Running from the cross will not only limit our spiritual growth, but it will also make us less effective as leaders and make our mission less fruitful.

—————————————— **DISCUSS** ——————————————

How are you tempted to evade the cross? In what ways do you struggle with self-seeking in mission rather than self-giving?

"GO OUT OF YOUR WAY IN SMALL MATTERS..."

In relationships, the most profound and lasting expressions of love are not found in occasional big things (like fancy dinners, adventures, diamonds, or vacations) but rather in the small, consistent acts of kindness — the little sacrifices, the little ways we put our beloved's needs, preferences and interests before our own.

The same is true in our relationship with Jesus. The real test of our enduring love for the Lord is not found in big moments, like how we felt close to him on a certain retreat or sporadic acts of generosity and service. Rather, the real test of a disciple is found in the many little acts of love and sacrifice we can offer our Lord each day.

Self-denial ... may be considered the test whether we are Christ's disciples."

— St. John Henry Newman

Consider how St. John Henry Newman encourages us to find little opportunities each day to deny ourselves and express our love for Jesus:

> Rise up early then in the morning with the purpose that (please God) the day shalt not pass without its self-denial. ... Let your very rising out of your bed be a self-denial; let your meals be self-denials. Determine to yield to others in things indifferent, to go out of your way in small matters, to inconvenience yourself. ... A man says to himself, "How am I to know I am in earnest?" I would suggest to him, Make some sacrifice, do some distasteful thing, which you are not actually obliged to do ... to bring home to your mind that in fact you do love your Saviour, that you do hate sin, that you do hate your sinful nature, that you have put aside the present world. Thus you will have an evidence (to a certain point) that you are not using mere words.[3]

Truly, truly, I say to you, unless a grain of wheat falls into the earth and dies, it remains alone; but if it dies, it bears much fruit."
— *John 12:24*

Someone who grows to the next level of love, to the next level of discipleship, goes out of their way to express love for Jesus each day in small matters. We can, for example, express our love in little acts of self-denial by fulfilling our duties in life: choosing to work on a paper even though we'd rather socialize some more; completing a difficult task in the office even though we'd rather do the easier projects first; stopping what we're doing at home to change a diaper or serve our spouse; being faithful to daily prayer even when we're stressed and busy. Fulfilling our basic commitments, even when inconvenient or uninteresting, is one crucial way of showing our love for God and neighbor.

We can also practice self-denial in our words: not dominating conversation, not talking about ourselves all the time, not gossiping or criticizing other people, not whining and complaining when things are hard ("I'm so tired"; "I'm hungry"; "I have so much to do!"; "This project is so difficult!"). These are small acts of love for Jesus and others that help strengthen community with others.

We can practice self-denial in our interactions with others. We can choose to be patient when others frustrate us, to forgive when others hurt us, and to be generous with our time when others need help. We can practice self-denial at table by fasting on occasion: not eating as much as we'd like, not eating between meals, or giving up our favorite food or drink. We can even practice self-denial with our screens: choosing not to waste time looking at our phones late at night or binge-watching our favorite show; choosing instead to give the best of ourselves to others and put our phones away when we're in conversation with them.

These are just a few examples of the many ways we can express our love through little acts of self-denial. The more we pick up our cross daily and follow Jesus, the more we will become like him and love like him. This is how we know that we are truly living as disciples (being "in earnest," as Cardinal Newman calls it): We are willing to embrace the cross.

––––––––––––––––––––– **DISCUSS** –––––––––––––––––––––

What is your attitude toward self-denial? In what ways do you practice self-denial regularly? In what areas of your life do you resist self-denial?

TAKE ACTION

As you seek to take on a new disposition toward self-denial and learn to embrace the crosses in your own life, the first step is to do some reflection. Set aside some time for prayer in which you examine the crosses in your life and reflect on how Jesus might be asking you to respond to them. Consider the following questions:

- In what ways is your spiritual life or your mission still focused on self, rather than on surrendering to Christ?

- Is your mission driven by love or by what you get out of it?

- Do you maintain relationships with those who are different from you or who may misunderstand your faith? Or do you choose to associate with those who are similar to you?

- When you encounter challenges in mission (people don't come to Bible study, people say no to the Gospel or to an invitation), do you get discouraged or tempted to give up? Or do you persevere and offer up the trials for love of souls?

- Do you attempt to hide from persecution or rejection, or do you continue to pursue others with a heart of love?

- Do you pray more for the various situations you want Jesus to change, or do you bring the darkened areas of your own heart to Jesus and allow him to transform them as he desires?

After your reflection, choose one way you can embrace these crosses and set a goal for how you will do that every day.

KEY CONCEPTS

Pick Up Your Cross: "If any man would come after me, let him deny himself and take up his cross daily and follow me" (Lk 9:23).

Law of Self-Giving: When we give of ourselves in love to God, to mission and to others, we don't lose anything, but our lives are deeply enriched and we gain so much more, for we are living according to the way God made us.

ADDITIONAL RESOURCES

A Witness to Joy by Servant of God Chiara Corbella Petrillo

CCC 599–618: "Christ's Redemptive Death in God's Plan of Salvation and Christ Offered Himself to His Father for Our Sins"

Notes

[1] Cicero, "In Defense of Rabirius," in *The Speeches of Cicero*, trans. H. Gross Hodge (Cambridge: Harvard, 1952), 467.

[2] Vatican Council II, *Gaudium Et Spes*, accessed February 12, 2020, Vatican.va, 24.

[3] St. John Henry Newman, "Sermon 5: Self-Denial, the Test of Religious Earnestness," *Newmanreader.org*, accessed February 10, 2020, http://www.newmanreader.org/works/parochial/volume1/sermon5.html.

Notes

Notes

FOCUS (Fellowship of Catholic University Students) is a Catholic apostolate whose mission is to share the hope and joy of the Gospel. FOCUS missionaries encounter people in friendship, inviting them into a personal relationship with Christ and accompanying them as they pursue lives of virtue and excellence. Through Bible studies, outreach events, mission trips, and discipleship, missionaries inspire and build up others in the faith, sending them out to live out lifelong Catholic mission wherever they are.

If you would like to know more about FOCUS, please visit www.focus.org or contact info@focus.org.

CURTIS MARTIN is the founder and CEO of the Fellowship of Catholic University Students (FOCUS), one of the fastest-growing apostolates in the Catholic Church. He holds a Master's degree in theology and is the author of several books, including the best-seller *Made for More*. Martin is a well-known Catholic speaker and served as co-host of the popular EWTN series *Crossing the Goal*. In 2011, Martin was appointed to serve as a Consultor to the Pontifical Council for Promoting the New Evangelization. He and his wife, Michaelann, live in Colorado. They have been blessed with nine children.

DR. EDWARD SRI is a theologian, author, and well-known Catholic speaker. He has written several best-selling books, including *Men, Women & the Mystery of Love*, *Walking with Mary*, and *Into His Likeness: Be Transformed as a Disciple*. He is also the presenter for the acclaimed film series *Symbolon: The Catholic Faith Explained*, and host of the weekly podcast "All Things Catholic." Dr. Sri is a founding leader with Curtis Martin of FOCUS, where he currently serves as Vice President of Formation. He and his wife Beth reside in Colorado and have eight children.

Looking for more great Catholic content on evangelization and discipleship?

Visit **www.focusequip.org**

YOU WILL FIND:

Bible Studies

Discipleship Resources

The FOCUS Blog

Video Resources

And More!

Visit the Foundations for Discipleship webpage for additional content, digital resources, and more!

Visit **www.focusequip.org/foundations**